Digital Storytelling, A Youth

MW01005601

Digital Storytelling, Applied Theatre, & Youth argues that theatre artists must reimagine how and why they facilitate performance practices with young people. Rapid globalization and advances in media and technology continue to change the ways that people engage with and understand the world around them. Drawing on pedagogical, aesthetic, and theoretical threads of applied theatre and media practices, this book presents practitioners, scholars, and educators with innovative approaches to devising and performing digital stories.

This book offers the first comprehensive examination of digital storytelling as an applied theatre practice. Alrutz explores how participatory and mediated performance practices can engage the wisdom and experience of youth; build knowledge about self, others, and society; and invite dialogue and deliberation with audiences. In doing so, she theorizes digital storytelling as a site of possibility for critical and relational practices, feminist performance pedagogies, and alliance building with young people.

Digital Storytelling, Applied Theatre, & Youth

Performing Possibility

Megan Alrutz

Routledge
Taylor & Francis Group

LONDON AND NEW YORK

First published 2015
by Routledge
2 Park Square, Milton Park, Abingdon, Oxon OX14 4RN

and by Routledge
711 Third Avenue, New York, NY 10017

Routledge is an imprint of the Taylor & Francis Group, an informa business

British Library Cataloguing in Publication Data
A catalogue record for this book is available from the British Library

Library of Congress Cataloging-in-Publication Data
A catalog record for this book has been requested

ISBN: 978-0-415-83218-2 (hbk)
ISBN: 978-0-415-83219-9 (pbk)
ISBN: 978-0-203-50060-6 (ebk)

Typeset in Sabon
by Taylor & Francis Books

Printed and bound in the United States of America by
Edwards Brothers Malloy on sustainably sourced paper

To Daniel and Grace, who make my everything possible

Contents

Figures and Tables

Figures

Tables

Acknowledgements

This book is inspired by my collaborations with many young people, teaching artists, scholars, community members, friends, and mentors. Among them, I am most grateful to Stephani Etheridge Woodson, who took a risk and invited a young practitioner into a world of digital technology, devising, and critically engaged dramaturgy, and Roger Bedard, who challenged me to trust my instincts and keep writing. Heartfelt thanks to Priscilla, Gus, Tiffany, Manny, Autumn, and all of the young people who shared their stories, hid my shoes, and took leaps of faith as I was getting started. I continue to learn from the questions, experiences, and wisdom you brought to our collaborations, as well as your invitation to reimagine what it means to be a youth-ally. Thanks also to my collaborators and colleagues at the University of Central Florida—Traci Reitz, Vandy Wood, Sybil St. Claire, and Paul Lartinoix—for encouraging my dream projects and nurturing a space for young people to explore digital storytelling and theatre.

More recently, my research for this project was well supported by the University of Texas at Austin and other Austin-based collaborators. Many thanks to Dean Dempster at the College of Fine Arts for supporting critical research leaves and funding the research necessary for completing this book. The Foxworth Centennial Fellowship and the Grace Hill Milam Centennial Fellowship offered much needed space for moving through this project, and I am thankful for the foresight, support, and recognition of these family foundations. I am equally grateful for the support from my colleagues in Drama & Theatre for Youth & Communities who continue to encourage my larger trajectory of work as an artist-scholar. Katie Dawson, Coleman Jennings, Joan Lazarus, Roxanne Schroeder-Arce, and Suzan Zeder—thank you for making the time and space for me to explore, research, dream, direct, and write. To my department mentor, Susan Mickey, I appreciate your support and advocacy at every turn. Paul Bonin-Rodriguez, Charlotte Canning, and Brant Pope have directly supported my work on this manuscript and continue to encourage my efforts to integrate theory and practice. I thank Kris Andrews and the Center for Educator Development; Amy Guadagnoli, Judy Jennings, and Resources for Learning; Tameika, Hannah, Benjamin, Lui, and Oliver. Each of these individuals and organizations provided me with critical opportunities and encouragement to experiment with digital technologies and performance with young people.

The ideas in this book are also influenced by my collaborations with past and present graduate students at the University of Texas at Austin and the University of Central Florida, as well as with many youths across the country. Sincere thanks to Alicia Fuss, Amanda Kibler, Amanda Morris, Amie Kisling, Cicely Bosley, Karen Weberman, Lucy Bryson, Meghann Henry, Meredith Hoppe, Nick Bazo, Katie Eckert, Rebecca Podsednik, Shelli Kinsley, Jennifer Adams, Rozz Grigsby, and many others—for experimenting with me, challenging me, and reminding me that artistry can and should be a relational practice. Anne McNamee, Michelle Dahlenburg, Meg Greene, Noah Martin, and Tallerie McRae—your work in digital and applied performance practices continues to deepen my thinking about the possibilities of this work with young people. Elizabeth Brendel Horn and Emily Freeman, I especially appreciate your research assistance on this book and your constant willingness to engage with me around the social, political, and practical underpinnings of applied theatre. Thank you all of my students for taking this journey with me.

I am also indebted to an amazing circle of women and men who continue to help me imagine feminist and anti-racist performance work with young people. To Kristen Hogan, my writing sister and friend, your wisdom, encouragement, and patience have been invaluable in my writing process and my life in general. Thank you for your endless readings, discussions, and feminist tables; you challenge me to see the world anew on a daily basis and to think deeply about arts as activism. Julia Listengarten, Amanda Hashagen, Roxanne Schroeder-Arce, Amy Jensen, and Lynn Hoare, I am deeply grateful for your willingness to read my raw materials and pose critical questions with a great deal of love. Your honest insights and your generous friendships make me a better scholar, teacher, and practitioner. Thanks also to Matt Richardson, Wura Ogunji, and Fiona Macbeth and Rebecca Rosser—our work together has seeped into these pages.

To my editors and readers on this project, I am grateful for your keen insights and constant encouragement. Ben Piggott and Harriet Affleck—thank you for championing this project. Your feedback was invaluable in places of struggle and delight, and you reminded me that meaningful projects require patience and time. To the four readers on this project—your feedback is also manifested in these pages. Thank you for providing me with critical maps and places for clarity, as well as bringing such a generous spirit to your reading of my work.

The cover photo for this book was generously provided by photographer Ethan Busse, a student of Youth in Focus (2013). Many thanks to Ethan and Youth in Focus, a nationally recognized youth development photography program, whose mission is to empower urban youth, through photography, to experience their world in new ways and to make positive choices for their lives (www.youthinfocus.org). Some of the ideas and stories in this book were first explored in articles that I published in *Teaching Artist Journal* (2006) and

Research in Drama Education: The Journal of Applied Theatre and Performance (2013). While the writing has been cited, revised, and/or expanded for this project, I would like to express my gratitude to *TAJ* and *RIDE*; the respective editors and reviewers of each journal undoubtedly shaped my current perspectives and writing about digital storytelling and applied theatre.

Finally, much love and gratitude to my family and friends, who continue to support my life and work in academia and theatre. This career is not always forgiving of everyday commitments and connections, and I thank you for your understanding and graciousness in my long and many absences. Daniel, Grace, Mom and Peter, Dad, Emily and Brian, Michael, Claire, Sean and Emily, Etta and Aubrey, Alyssa and Tad, Grandma and Grandpa, Shannon and Ricky, Carmen, Rick, Sonny, Maggie, Joaquin, and Davy and Marisol, please know that you helped bring this book to fruition. I feel your support, love, and encouragement always, but especially over the last several years.

Preface

Toward the end of writing this book, I experienced a pretty profound moment of seeing myself in and through someone else's digital story. My dad emailed me a link to a trailer for a documentary called *American Commune*. The trailer features two grown sisters, now documentarians, revisiting their childhood on one of the largest intentional living communities in the United States, called The Farm. The sisters left The Farm around the same time my own family did, and the trailer suggests that the transition was fraught with complications, tensions, and questions around their non-traditional upbringing and the unrealized ideals put forth by the community. As adults, the sisters travel back to The Farm and explore the "rise and fall of America's largest utopian social experiment" (*American Commune*), all through the frame of their deeply personal life stories or relationships to this place.

In truth, this digital story surprised me. Or maybe my reaction to it surprised me. I was filled with memories, associations, and stories from my own life—growing up on The Farm and later struggling as a young child to integrate into public school and many other aspects and expectations of US society I encountered when my family reintegrated into mainstream society. I watched the trailer multiple times and experienced moments of delight, grief, disbelief, and finally understanding. The sisters sounded and in some ways looked like me. Their vocabulary included what I call "hippy talk," and their childhood photos showed awkward girls in bare feet and tie-dyed T-shirts. Their experiences felt familiar and their journey reminded me of my own. I did not know these sisters, and yet in some ways I felt I knew them well. Seeing this story, hearing the very words the sisters used to describe their childhood, and thinking about their perspectives helped me see how and why I move through the world in my particular way. Their story made me think about my relationship to people, power, and authority, and ultimately why I continue to pursue applied theatre and digital storytelling with young people.

I grew up within a significant movement toward a self-sustainable, vegan lifestyle and a non-traditional paradigm for living and working in community. From a very young age, I was surrounded with stories, experiences, and narratives about community responsibility and social justice. I lived closely with thousands of people who moved to rural Tennessee to work the land and create a non-violent, non-commercial, and environmentally and spiritually responsible society. Residents took a lifelong vow of poverty, sharing simple housing and self-grown food, and rejecting makeup, jewelry, and other forms of material wealth and vanity. Growing up in this setting, I learned that I was responsible for creating a more just planet, that all people deserved respect and freedom from violence, and that I was part of something larger than myself.

I was also immersed in communal living. We lived with several families in a single home with no hot running water or indoor toilets. Food was rationed to each household and everyone pitched in to cook, clean, and care for the kids. Although the commune aimed to employ people's passions and skills, in some ways, little room existed for individualism and it was frowned upon to *get into the juice*, which meant doing anything that might be perceived as complaining or taking focus from the group. Watching the trailer for *American Commune*, I became hyper aware of how these life experiences now align with and push against my current politics. My personal narratives about social change and political responsibility sometimes collide with my desire to keep the peace and to avoid *getting into the juice*. My history—including my family and community narratives—manifest daily in my efforts to live and work as a social justice ally. They also explicitly shape my own messy relationship to relational and justice-oriented performance practices with young people.

This book grows out of my life experiences, stories, and research. But, at its core, this book and its ideas are inspired by my collaborations with smart, brave, and creative young people. Youths on the Gila River Indian Community in Bapchule, AZ, taught me that media and technology can sometimes prove more accessible than live performance and that young people need to tell stories on their own terms. A group of young women in Orlando, FL, showed me the importance of sharing stories within a community of practice, and not simply for an audience. A group of LGBTQ youth in Austin, TX, reminded me that if and when we fail to address the politics of narrative, our silence signals complicity. I am grateful to each of them—for their stories and for their willingness to engage with me in this life work and passion. Each of these young people helps me know and understand that listening to, imagining, and telling stories creates possibilities—for seeing ourselves, each other, and a more just society.

References

American Commune *Synopsis*, <http://www.americancommunemovie.com/film-synopsis/> (accessed July 21, 2013).

1 Digital storytelling as an applied theatre praxis

Power on the line: personal narratives move people

Possibility: a future prospect or potential.

Several years ago, I answered my office phone to a concerned citizen yelling at me. "How dare you!" she said. "I can't believe that you have the nerve to spend my tax dollars on theatre and media programs for those kids—those kids whose parents are prostitutes and liars and drug addicts. Why should *they* get special treatment—special arts programs? There are a lot of other kids, good kids, that deserve that platform." In part, the caller made a solid point—lots of other kids do deserve that platform. Applied theatre and digital media programs can and should offer many communities of youth opportunities to participate in socially valuable arts practices.

My anonymous caller, uninterested in a dialogue, eventually hung up on me. Although listening to her monologue proved challenging, her narrative pushed me to revisit how and why performing one's personal story matters. To tell your story for a public audience, to share your (perhaps marginalized, new, unpopular, or uncomfortable) narrative, can have the potential to affect how each of us, the teller and the collective "us," sees the past, participates in the present, and imagines the future. Performance asserts the value of individuals and their experiences. Moreover, performance can constitute both the making and the disruption of systems of power.

The youth referred to by my caller were involved in Digital U, a community-based digital storytelling program that I co-directed out of the University of Central Florida with media artist Traci Reitz. Over the course of three years, we employed applied theatre and digital media forms to engage youth participants in creating digital stories—or short, personally narrated movies and digital performance collages about and relevant to their lives. The process and the products of this embodied and technologically mediated performance program intentionally worked to disrupt hegemonic narratives about youth identity. As with my call, every so often, the politics of applied theatre can become amplified in public discourse. The tensions around the foregrounding of marginalized youth voices made me reflect more fully on the value of critical representational practices and on the complex relationships between youth, media, performance, and power.

Digital Storytelling, Applied Theatre, & Youth: Performing Possibility grows out of these and other recent reflections, and more specifically from my desire to query digital storytelling and applied theatre as sites of possibility for valuing the experiences and wisdom of young people.[1]

My research as an artist-scholar over the last twelve-plus years has focused on critical pedagogy and issues of responsible representation in applied theatre, digital storytelling, arts integration, and theatre for young audiences. This book builds on and extends my previous work to include critical considerations of technologies of engagement in applied theatre settings, specifically as tools for performing identity, enacting social change, and addressing identity-based inequities. Moreover, it draws on my research and practice as a director of various applied theatre and digital media programs in school and community-based settings, as well as on my work as a graduate student at Arizona State University (Tempe, AZ), where my studies in theatre for youth deepened my exposure to embodied, engaged, and critical performance pedagogies and practices.

While at Arizona State University, I worked as the resident teaching artist for two years in a community-based digital storytelling and performance residency program called Place: Vision & Voice (PVV). I collaborated with the program director Stephani Etheridge Woodson to facilitate digital storytelling performance programs foregrounding the thoughts and experiences of youth participants within their schools, communities, and society at large. I began exploring the relationships between photography, video, and performance, and I experimented with embodied and media-based approaches to engaging youth and devising stories. The program worked toward public showings of students' work and often framed significant community conversations about the topics raised in the digital stories themselves. While the youths in PVV created and reflected on their own mediated—or digitally rendered—representations, we placed little emphasis on technical proficiency with digital editing, and the students relied on us to physically put all of the pieces together into a final product. Working from students' loosely constructed storyboards and responding to their feedback on the digitally documented products, I learned to edit their digital assets (voiceovers, music, photographs, and digital video) into completed digital stories. This process of negotiation and performance-making with youths gave me insight into how personal agency, or the ability to represent self or enact change, can increase with technical proficiency in digital media production.

Years later, as a faculty member at the University of Central Florida, I co-developed Digital U, a program that housed several long-term digital storytelling and applied theatre initiatives focused on creative approaches to integrating technology, arts, and education. Drawing on my experience with critical drama-based pedagogy and digital storytelling, the Digital U initiatives worked to foster a supportive community in which young people could practice self-expression and community advocacy. I continued to explore the possibility of a program model that supported the youth agency that can come with technical savvy and also built visual literacy and community-engagement skills among the participants. Although we emphasized the technical skills needed to create and edit one's own digital media products from start to finish, sometimes we achieved this at the expense of intentionally facilitating community dialogue or equipping participants to create a unified visual aesthetic within their digital stories. With Digital U, we did not always attend to critical, drama-based practice or create the conditions for sustaining community dialogues. Moreover, I struggled with how or why the significance or impact of a digital story might move beyond the individual's experience of creation.

My work in PVV and Digital U raised questions around how to combine embodied and mediated representational practices with greater attention to the relationship between form and function in performance. Drawing on theory and practice from both applied theatre and digital storytelling, I began to imagine new ways of enacting and facilitating performance work with young people. After joining the faculty at the University of Texas at Austin, I partnered with colleagues to build two new applied performance programs underpinned by critical and engaged pedagogies: Inside OUT[2] and the Performing Justice Project[3] (PJP). With each of these programs, my partners and I aim to facilitate a critically engaged performance practice that attends to issues of identity and power through a variety of applied theatre and digital storytelling strategies. I am more attuned to the ways technology serves as a tool for performing and staging creative expression. In many ways, digital editing parallels the work of theatre directors, designers, and dramaturges who consider how best to communicate the core of any story. Similarly, taking a photograph invites us to think like theatre artists—to analyze and communicate characters, relationships, and power, as well as points of view and objectives. Making choices around the use of music and video for a digital story parallels working with or as a designer or director; we consider ways to communicate mood, movement, and an emotional arc. Digital storytelling relies on a plethora of skills that we already use to create and tell clear stories on stage and in applied theatre settings. However, with these more recent programs, I am building on the work of applied theatre with youth to intentionally blend embodied and mediated forms and to explore the relationships between youth, identity, and justice.

Inside OUT and PJP continue to build on the assets, capacities, and interests of youth participants and community partners. The resulting performance products and the processes involved to create them reveal new sites of possibility that require further research and attention. Like digital storytelling as an applied theatre practice, this book invites artists, teachers, scholars, and communities to consider the possibilities, tensions, and politics of youth performance in new ways. As you read this book, I invite you to imagine how the integration of embodied and mediated performance can deepen our future engagements with youth and communities.

Generative intersections: digital storytelling and applied theatre

Rapid globalization and advances in media and technology continue to change the ways that youth engage with and understand the world around them.

Moreover, as digital technologies become more accessible and central to everyday life, artists face new challenges around engaging communities in live theatre events and facilitating performance practices that prove relevant to youth's lived experiences. These shifts around technology, and the challenges they present, invite applied theatre practitioners to develop and engage with new approaches to performance that better reflect and respond to the lives of our participants.

With this book, I give attention to the generative intersections of applied theatre and digital storytelling and explore how particular live and mediated performance practices create new sites of possibility around youth participation and representation. The intersections of these practices present unique and under-theorized opportunities for addressing current issues, such as my own concerns around the relevance and accessibility of theatre to young people today and the representations of, with, and for young people. Various forms of digital media and technology have become increasingly accessible to "ordinary people," offering applied theatre artists innovative tools for engaging youth and communities in performance work. Specifically, I name and examine digital storytelling as an applied theatre practice as a site for addressing three spaces of possibility:

- the engagement and valuing of youth in society
- the creation of new knowledge around self, others, and society
- the fostering of dialogue and action around issues of identity, culture, and community.

With the increasing popularity of technology in our everyday lives, I am interested in how we can harness the potential and negotiate the challenges of digital media in and through the performance of personal stories. Through attention to how we value and engage youth, build new knowledge, and foster dialogue and change, I examine how this interdisciplinary practice invites participants to contribute to and critique systems of power in their lives. What can embodied and mediated performance teach us about young people and their ideas for the future? How can digital storytelling and applied theatre combine to develop and shift our understandings of who we are and our place in the world? In what ways does the intentional performance and dissemination of digital stories enact young people's vision of themselves and their lives? And finally, how do our embodied and mediated performance practices work together to disrupt, re-vision, and reify[4] ideas about young people, identity, and society? Working from the premise that young people benefit from opportunities to imagine, reflect on, and re-vision their future, I problematize these and other sites of struggle and opportunity to present new approaches to collaborating with youths and actively pursuing a more just and equitable world.

Digital storytelling as an applied theatre practice foregrounds youth's lived experiences and capitalizes on their relationship to media and technology, as well as their desire for meaningful interactions with each other, adults, and community. By attending to pedagogical, aesthetic, and theoretical threads of both digital storytelling and applied theatre, I outline practical frameworks for devising, performing, and disseminating digital stories with youth. Furthermore, I draw on critically engaged pedagogy and performance, as well as applied theatre and media theory, to offer performance practices that aim to shift the ways that young people see themselves, as well as the ways we value them in schools, communities, and society at large.

Digital storytelling: a brief overview

Digital storytelling has garnered much attention from media artists, community organizers, and scholars since the early 1990s as a process for engaging marginalized voices in the social/cultural economy of the media. The term digital storytelling encompasses a wide range of self-produced media—such as blogs and podcasts—that employ story and digital technologies for personal expression. In a strict sense, though, and more to the topic of this book, digital storytelling refers to the creation of short digital videos, or two- to three-minute personal stories performed through a combination of first-person, narrated voiceovers; still and/or moving images; and music or sound. This specific genre of digital storytelling was formally developed and promoted by media producers and artists Joe Lambert and the late Dana Atchley who, together with Nina Mullen, founded the Center for Digital Storytelling (formerly the San Francisco Digital Media Center) in Berkley, CA, in 1994. The Center's well-documented and globally implemented digital storytelling process aims to democratize media production by guiding non-professionals to produce (rather than simply consume) mediatized stories about their own lives (Center 2011: History; Hartley and McWilliams 2009; Lambert 2009, 2010).

The Center for Digital Storytelling's (CDS) aims and projects are rooted in cultural democracy and community arts, as well as popular education movements in the United States (Center 2011: History). On their website, the CDS is defined as "an international nonprofit training, project development, and research organization that assists youth and adults around the world in using digital media tools to craft and record meaningful stories from their lives and share these stories in ways that enable learning, build community, and inspire justice" (Center 2011: home page). Joe Lambert cites connections between digital storytelling and the work of Arlene Goldberg and Jan Cohen-Cruz, among other artist-scholars whose work continues to influence community arts and applied theatre practices.

Digital storytelling has become an international movement of sorts, now utilized by libraries, schools, museums, and other cultural and business institutions to engage and interact with their constituents (Hartley and McWilliams 2009; Hill and Vasudevan 2008; Lundby 2008). Moreover, activists and community workers around the world employ the CDS's process to support community cultural initiatives, public and community health goals, and international development efforts (Center 2011: *Evolution*). A significant body of research is also emerging on digital storytelling efforts in education and community-based settings with youth, as well as on digital storytelling as a pedagogy, or a process for meaningful teaching and learning (Goodman 2003; Gustavson 2008; Hartley and McWilliam 2009; Hill and Vasudevan 2008; Hull and Katz 2006; Lambert 2009, 2010; McGeoch and Hughes 2009). However, despite the many parallels between digital storytelling, theatre and drama, and applied theatre and performance, little writing exists on digital stories by youth as a performance itself or on how applied theatre and digital storytelling practices might benefit from one another.[5]

Applied drama and theatre: a brief overview

Applied drama and theatre (ADT) is an umbrella term widely used to describe a variety of theatre and drama practices that take place in educational, social, and community-based settings with aims that extend beyond theatre production itself. In ADT, performance is used as a means for social, cultural, political, educational, and personal change (Cohen-Cruz 2005; Nicholson 2005; Prendergast and Saxton 2009; Prentki and Preston 2009; Taylor 2003; Thompson 2003). Prentki and Preston suggest that although theatre processes are applied in the service of self-development, well-being, and social change within ADT, the "intent is subject to differing interpretation and understanding by practitioners, and is influenced by context and the social, cultural or political landscapes which shape the artistic interventions that are created" (2009: 14). ADT focuses on local and community interests, as well as engaging individuals and groups with little to no formal training in the arts. Across the wide range of practices, participants, and intentions, ADT facilitators guide participants through a collaborative and interactive process of examining questions, themes, or concerns within and through performance and embodied self-expression. These contexts support a performance practice that is simultaneously engaged, social, and artistic (Prendergast and Saxton 2009).

ADT continues to garner discussion and debate, starting with, but not limited to, tensions around terminology and definition.[6] ADT scholar Helen Nicholson suggests that while the terms "applied drama" and "applied theatre" sometimes are used interchangeably, applied drama often suggests a process-based performance practice that does not result in a performance for an audience (2005). "Applied theatre, on the other hand, begins as a process but denotes a public or semi-public performance as a necessary component" (Prendergast and Saxton 2009: vi). For this book, I use the term applied theatre to reference a dynamic collection of performance tools, such as improvisation, storytelling, devising, image work, interactive theatre, and other engaged performance practices such as arts integration, theatre of the oppressed, theatre-in-education (TIE), and museum theatre. I use applied theatre and its related terminology to emphasize a process-oriented approach to performance that may or may not involve a presentation for an outside audience, but that ultimately works toward an intentionally framed performance—if only for the participants themselves—coupled with guided reflection and dialogue of some kind.

Applied theatre is interdisciplinary in that it is both applied to and draws on many areas of practice. Like digital storytelling, applied theatre has roots in the community arts movement and works to democratize social and cultural production through direct participation in art-making. Prendergast and Saxton suggest that applied theatre also grows out of movements in popular theatre, theatre-in-education, and theatre of the oppressed (2009), while Prentki and Preston demonstrate its links to grassroots and community-based theatre, problem-posing and progressive education, and theatre for development (TfD) (2009). Building on the ideological underpinnings of each of these movements, applied theatre often attends to ideas and questions related to community, education, and participation, as well as power and activism. For this book, I draw on many of these practical and theoretical traditions to build an applied theatre praxis that is anchored in a critical, drama-based pedagogy with and for young people.

Untapped potential: integrating applied theatre and digital storytelling

Digital storytelling and applied theatre share many parallels in their history, form, and function. They also complement each other, offering opportunities to combine differing practices, as well as intentions, goals, and outcomes to create a dynamic and multilayered approach to performance. In Table 1.1, I offer a brief introduction to the relationship between these two fields, touching on what I see as key areas of intersection within each practice, including the history and roots of the work; typical or targeted participants; nature and structure of participation; creative process (with attention to preparation, production/devising, and presentation); and performance (with attention to products and mediums). Through a side-by-side comparison, Table 1.1 suggests opportunities for combining these two practices to offer young people an interdisciplinary, critically engaged, and multimodal approach to performance.

As digital media becomes increasingly woven into the fabric of our lives, young people readily invite the language of interactive technologies into our creative spaces, forcing a reconsideration of what constitutes theatre and performance. Digital media—specifically digital storytelling—has the potential to extend and deepen our work as applied theatre artists. Similarly, applied theatre offers alternative approaches to engaging young people in the making of media and the performance of personal story.

According to Joe Lambert, digital storytelling grows out of efforts to situate digital media production in the hands of "common folk" (2009: 79). The CDS, and subsequent groups promoting similar methodologies, move digital media production into community-based settings and work to engage the general public in representational practices traditionally reserved for elite groups or highly trained media specialists (Lambert 2009, 2010). Despite its success in achieving these ends, digital storytelling (and information technology in general) continues to garner criticism for its focus on

Table 1.1 Overview of Digital Storytelling and Applied Theatre

	Digital Storytelling	Applied Theatre
History/roots	Community arts movement Digital, media, and visual arts Live theatre and performance Storytelling Oral history Progressive education Community cultural development Cultural democracy Media literacy Technology education	Community arts movement Community-based theatre Grassroots theatre Popular theatre Theatre for social change Theatre for development (TfD) Theatre in education (TIE) Theatre of the oppressed Critical pedagogy Progressive and problem-posing education
Participants	Non-professional media specialists and "ordinary people" Often focuses on individuals with little or no experience with digital media or storytelling Sometimes engages marginalized or oppressed individuals	Non-professional theatre artists and non-actors Often focuses on individuals with little or no experience with theatre Often engages marginalized, underserved, or oppressed individuals and communities
Participation	Often short-term workshops: 3–5 days Some long-term projects that engage a series of individuals over time Technologically engaged with elements of cooperative, social interaction Fluid, improvisational, and collaborative	Often long-term, ongoing partnerships, programs, or projects that occur over a series of weeks, months, or years Some short-term workshops: 1–3 days Interactive, social, and cooperative Reflective and reflexive
Structure	Focused on individuals' personal experiences and stories Attention given to the group process through story circles and feedback from participants	Focused on a group devising processes rooted in participants' ideas Attention given to individuals' stories, perspectives, experiences, and identities

	Digital Storytelling	Applied Theatre
	Individuals are responsible for the production of their own digital story in a collaborative environment Digital storytelling facilitators guide individuals to share, listen, revise, storyboard, represent, and edit their digital stories Digital storytelling facilitators screen the products for the group of participants	Personal reflections and experiences contribute to a group image, idea, or understanding Small or whole groups are responsible for the devising of their performance pieces Applied theatre facilitator guides the group(s) to devise, share, reflect on, and re-vision their embodied images, improvisations, and performance pieces The group may or may not create formal performance pieces for an outside audience
Process: preparation	Individuals bring pre-prepared personal stories and photographs to a digital storytelling workshop Participants watch digital stories and analyze them for Lambert's seven elements of, or seven steps for creating, a digital story[a] Individuals share their narratives in a story circle and receive feedback from peers and facilitators	Facilitator guides a group of individuals through a series of theatre exercises to build trust and a sense of ensemble and collaborative play Group of participants use embodied image work, improvisation, theatre games, and activities to explore and determine issues and questions relevant to individuals and the group at large
Process: production	Individuals work in pairs to further revise personal stories and script their voice-over narratives Individuals storyboard, or map out a plan for weaving visual and audio elements together with their voice-overs Individuals create or secure visual assets, including photographs, images, and video clips Individuals record a voice-over of their narrative and secure other audio assets, such as sound effects and music	Whole groups or small subset groups of participants explore a determined theme, issue, or question Participants collaboratively devise live and embodied performance pieces, such as monologues, scenes, images, movement sequences, soundscapes, and other physical and vocal improvisations Facilitator guides participants to share their work with the larger group of participants

(continued)

Table 1.1 Overview of Digital Storytelling and Applied Theatre (*continued*)

	Digital Storytelling	Applied Theatre
	Individuals use editing software to combine layers of visual text, recorded narrative, and sound or music into a completed digital story	Facilitator guides participants to connect individual experiences to that of the group through reflections on the work created
Process: presentation	Digital stories are projected on or played through a screen Digital stories are screened among the participants of the group Digital stories may be presented in a live or virtual environment, for a live or virtual audience, and can live on through the Internet and other digital environments or archives Products may or may not be shared with an audience beyond the participant group	Applied theatre may or may not include a formally produced presentation Products are performed by live people for a live audience in a variety of informal or formal venues Performances generally do not emphasize high production values, such as costumes, lighting, or sets A live performance is shared with an invited or targeted audience, or individuals otherwise invested in the topic at hand Performances often include elements of audience participation or interaction Facilitator guides audience to connect their individual experiences to that of the group to focus on the need or opportunities for change
Performance medium	Technologically mediated (performed through photography, video, and recorded voice-over) Usually includes background music and/or sound effects May include literal and abstract representations	Live and embodied (performed in real time through body, face, and voice) May include elements of technology, such as lighting, music, or projections to support the performance

Performance products	DVD or other digital renderings of individual digital stories Stories can live on in the virtual world and digital archives (through platforms such as YouTube, Intersect, and personal websites)	Includes literal and abstract representations Live and embodied play, performance, or sharing of elements of the process May be shared or performed for the participant group and/or a wider public or semi-public audience Ephemeral (although audiences often take away concrete reflections, goals, or ideas for change)
Goals/outcomes	Democratize cultural production (or give people the opportunity and skills to create their own media products) Value personal experience and memory Enable learning Build community Knowledge management Personalize marketing and branding	Inspire people to imagine and enact social, cultural, political, educational, and personal change Value marginalized and underrepresented voices, perspectives, experiences, and ideas Educate and liberate Build community Support or disrupt the status quo Foster interaction, community dialogue, reflection Inspire action and justice

[a] Joe Lambert puts forth seven steps (formally "elements" in earlier publications) of digital story, namely, owning your insights; owning your emotions; finding the moment; seeing your story; hearing your story; assembling your story; sharing your story (2010). The seven elements described in the first and second editions of his book included point of view; a dramatic question; emotional content; the gift of your voice; soundtrack; economy; and pacing (2006).

the individual user and sometimes-isolated expressions of personal concerns and perspectives.

Similarly, media education and media literacy programs designed for youth have been challenged for promoting a protectionist agenda, or narrowly focusing on the development of educated consumers (Goodman 2003; Hill and Vasudevan 2008), rather than "agentive selves" (Hull and Katz 2006) who also act as critical producers of their own media. Social and participatory media scholars Jerry Watkins and Angelina Russo point to a need for interactive digital practices that intentionally "respond to an ongoing debate" in society and focus on furthering human relationships (Watkins and Russo 2009: 271). Lambert also suggests that the digital storytelling process could benefit from lessened time constraints and more attention to the development of self-agency, social agency, and broader social awareness (2009: 89).

In many ways, applied theatre is uniquely situated to respond to these challenges. As a social and collaborative art form, applied theatre invites participants to perform and present stories of their own making. Nicholson argues that in theatre, knowledge—or meaning-making—is inherently "embodied, culturally located and socially distributed" (2005: 39). In other words, the personal and interactive nature of applied theatre works to construct and perform relationships between self, others, and society. While applied theatre draws on individual experiences and cultures, it also relies on group participation and the building of an intentional community of collaborators. Applied theatre also works to increase understanding and build dialogue, if not alliances, specifically among its collaborators and often with a larger group of participant-observers or audiences as well.

Bethany Nelson's applied theatre scholarship speaks to Hull and Katz's (2006) notion of agentive selves. She suggests, "The community-rich environment of [applied theatre] is uniquely well-positioned to facilitate the development of a sense of power in students and a capacity to act on and change their world" (2011: 166). In applied theatre settings, youth are invited to participate as creators, decision makers, and leaders. Rooted in Paulo Freire's critical pedagogy, applied theatre often invites youth to explore and reflect on how their choices and actions affect themselves and others, and ultimately shape outcomes, including the creative process, group dynamics, community dialogue, and performance pieces or products. As part of a collaborative and creative community, youth learn that they can and do impact, if not transform, themselves, the group, and sometimes society at large. Together, digital storytelling and applied theatre can create conditions for developing aspects of agency.

Digital storytelling as an applied theatre praxis

Weaving digital storytelling and applied theatre together responds to many of the criticisms waged against digital media, as well as the need for applied theatre artists to explore the role of technology and visual/screen literacy in our work with youth. When framed as an applied theatre praxis, digital storytelling invites participants to engage in a process of reflection and action or, as Nicholson says of applied theatre, "a cyclical process in which practice generates new insights and where, reciprocally, theoretical ideas are interrogated, created and embodied in practice" (2005: 39). Moreover, locating digital storytelling as an applied theatre praxis emphasizes the role of collaboration, cooperation, and dialogue. Personal narratives are placed in conversation with one another and often within the context of larger community and societal questions and debates—both during the creative process and through a facilitated dissemination of the performance work as well. Engaging in an applied theatre praxis also means valuing the ideas and input of the participants, emphasizing collaborative discovery and revision, and creating a space for reciprocity between participants, facilitators, and audiences of the work. This pairing shifts the focus from what could be a traditional (product-centered or director-driven) creative process to include embodied explorations with a self-reflective, interactive, and critically conscious lens.[7]

At its core, this book proposes a new creative process, drawing on these values and simultaneously privileging digital storytelling and applied theatre pedagogy and practice. With each project I work on, I shift my practices to accommodate the specific participants and contexts at hand. In addition, the young people with whom I work continue to inform my thinking about this interdisciplinary performance approach. While valuing the flexibility and improvisation afforded by this practice, I continue to ground my approach in three core principles:

1. The form is embodied and mediated.

2. The approach is critically engaged.

3. The practice makes explicit the values, experiences, and wisdom of young people.

Specifically, digital storytelling as an applied theatre practice relies on the intentional integration of live performance-making with digital representations. The process and products include real-time, embodied theatre and interactive performance elements, as well as digitally mediated representations such as photography, stop-animation, recorded voice-overs, and video. The approach is critically engaged, in that it brings attention to issues of power, identity, and inequity.

Drawing on critically engaged pedagogies and performance put forth by theorists such as Paolo Freire (1969), bell hooks (1994), Joe L. Kincheloe (2004), and Jan Cohen-Cruz (2010), my approach is underpinned by democratic participation, reciprocity, agency, and dialogue. My practical and theoretical frameworks emphasize relational practices and the building of alliances. Moreover, my approach encourages facilitators and participants to engage in critically reflective representational practices. In this way, I aim to foster accountability and responsibility to self, others, and community; the work supports participants to make choices through an analytical and creative process that considers outcomes and consequences of the work. Finally, in tandem with its form and approach, I focus on how performance practices work to value young people in creative spaces, local communities, and society at large. As such, the process remains fluid and open-ended, responding directly to the needs and desires of the youth participants, as well as new ideas and contexts that arise during or as a result of the creative process.

Mediated representations: benefits of an integrated praxis

Situating digital storytelling as an applied theatre praxis offers youth participants ways of seeing, constructing, and responding to the world. The theory and practice of this interdisciplinary performance work challenges traditional boundaries between youth as consumers and youth as producers. Together, applied theatre and digital storytelling encourage young people, and the artists who work with them, to become critically engaged "prosumers,"[8] or individuals who create products, ideas, and culture that they wish to consume, while attending to how power functions in representation. In this sense, the devising process and performance products function as political acts of cultural production. They offer young people an opportunity to reflect and archive—(re)vision and (re)construct—complex notions of (their) identity, culture, and community.

In my own practice, digital storytelling also diversifies youth participation in applied theatre. The addition of media-based performance tools draws in youths whose interests lie in digital media, visual art, film and television, animation, photography, and information technology—youths who might otherwise not join a theatre or performance program. Digital storytelling also offers twenty-first-century tools, such as digital photography, video, and visual collage, for engaging youth in a variety of performance practices. In addition, the merging of applied theatre and digital storytelling practices allows me to engage young people who might typically be excluded from the privilege of regular, ongoing participation in ensemble-based work. Digital storytelling, for example, is well situated to support the participation of migrant farmworkers and other transient populations without the luxury of time in any given place, as well as youth in foster care and others for whom staging the live body/voice for a public audience might carry high levels of risk. While digital media is not without its challenges around access, quality, and sustainability, it presents and extends performance opportunities as applied artists consider possibilities for engaging with and in the lives of young people.

Digital storytelling, as a performance process and medium, invites participants to reflect and archive, as well as (re)vision and construct, complex notions of who they are in the world. Leif Gustavson references Paul Willis's notion of a "grounded aesthetic," or "the everyday application of symbolic creativity … to common concerns and issues" (2008: 82; Willis 1998: 173), to demonstrate how visual and creative practices underpin young people's everyday lives. Gustavson further argues that to comprehend "how youth understand and live in the world, we need to shift our focus away from the products they consume or make (e.g., CDs, websites, jewelry) to the 'social practice' of making these products" (2008: 82). In other words, we must attend not simply to what youth consume and produce but also to how youth engage with each other and the world around them.

Framing digital storytelling as an applied theatre praxis foregrounds human relationships. This framework can also alert young people to the ways that collaborative media- and performance-making can become intentional, political acts of cultural production—a process from which youth are often excluded. This interdisciplinary praxis offers a performance process and product that examines and acts on systems of power and oppression that directly shape our lives. Devising performance and sharing stories in this way challenges and supports youth to (re)assemble, literally re-member, experiences and narratives in their lives. This creative act can inform not only how youth view themselves but also how their communities view youth, contributing to new relationships between young people, communities, and society at large.

Attending to youth stories: preparation, production, and presentation

As an applied theatre artist engaged with digital media, I focus on devising and performing personal stories and community narratives with young people. The applied theatre process activates personal stories of the group, as well as possibilities for building collaborative communities of practice and enacting social justice envisioned by youth participants. Moreover, digital storytelling, when coupled with applied theatre, invites youth to reflect on and (re)imagine meta-narratives about their lives. These possibilities present themselves throughout various stages of the creative process: preparation, production, and presentation. These stages map out the overarching creative process, pointing to a beginning, middle, and end; however, they also suggest a micro-process of devising new work, which often gets repeated as youth engage in a long-term performance-making process. Youth may prepare, produce, and present creative work again and again as they create a digital story, even if the work is never shown outside of their participant group. Importantly, while naming distinct parts of the process can help communicate how one moves through a creative process, these distinctions can fail to acknowledge that in fact the categories of preparation, production, and presentation often blur and share many elements in common.

For the sake of clarity, I offer a somewhat linear, facilitated process in each chapter of this book. The next three chapters address what I think are important possibilities for facilitating this work with youth. While at times I attend to these possibilities through examples from a particular stage in the creative process, these possibilities can and do occur throughout the creative process. Through this intentional practice, I work to value and engage young people, support the development of new knowledge and meaning-making, and foster reflection, dialogue, and deliberation at every stage of the process.

My approach to performance work with youth focuses on devising narratives, images, and story through theatre and digital media; however, the tangible product—the digital story itself—often comes late in the process and usually when the participants themselves determine a necessity or benefit of sharing their performance pieces with a larger public or semi-public audience. As an applied theatre artist, I strive to structure a collaborative, creative practice that engages, names, and honors participants' lived experiences and contributes to socially/culturally responsible performance-making. Once the digital stories are fully realized, we further examine possibilities for enacting justice, both within our participant group, as well as for outside audiences. We discuss external audiences who might engage with, or benefit from, seeing the piece(s), and work together to decide if/how a digital story or collection of digital stories might be performed or distributed. The creation of digitally devised and performed stories has significantly shifted my own applied theatre praxis to include both embodied and mediated elements of performance, digital artifacts, and face-to-face performance events and community conversations. These artifacts, and the circumstances and values surrounding their creation and dissemination, invite youth to simultaneously see themselves perform, and see themselves be performed—all within a context that they shape, contribute to, and/or direct.

In the chapters that follow, I offer some of the ways that this interdisciplinary work can support youth, and the teaching artists who work with them, to reflect on, create, and contribute to their wider cultural landscapes right now. Chapter 2 ("Engaging the Wisdom and Experience of Youth") argues that we must develop new ways to engage the ideas, experiences, and ingenuities of young people as we work toward a more just, equitable, and inclusive society. I explore what it means to become a youth-allied adult and how to support young people to engage in a collaborative community. I also offer aesthetic and pedagogical strategies for examining personal identity and inviting youth to confidently bring their lived experiences to a community of practice. Finally, this chapter demonstrates how facilitating digital storytelling as an applied theatre praxis can engage and value youth as agentive selves (Hull and Katz 2006) who both participate in, and contribute to, society.

Chapters 3 and 4 further address the production and presentation of digital stories through an applied theatre framework. In Chapter 3 ("Building Knowledge about Self, Others, and Society"), I explore how a critically engaged, performance pedagogy can support youth in tackling issues of inequity based in race, ethnicity, gender identity, sexuality, class, and dis/ability. This chapter investigates how the complex practice of producing digital stories (specifically, the devising, naming, representing, and exchanging of personal stories, through embodied performance, recorded voice-overs, digital photography, and video) offers a powerful process for seeing and naming, reflecting on, and re-visioning ideas about ourselves, others, and society. Moreover, this chapter demonstrates how working within a community of practice to create performance pieces ultimately supports youth in gathering and testing creative ideas, as well as making meaning about the world around them.

Chapter 4 ("Inviting Dialogue and Deliberation with Audiences") looks at how the presentation, specifically an intentional and participatory dissemination of digital stories, provides a platform for examining meta-narratives about youth and youth culture, identity politics, and society at large. I theorize that the sharing of, and reflecting on, digital stories with an audience through various participatory frames can invite youth to experience the power and (sometimes challenging/risky) potential of personal story and mediated performance to spark dialogue and deliberation, as well as to advocate for change or action on behalf of themselves and their communities.

In the last chapter ("Performing Possibility"), I reflect on some of the challenges of critical approaches to digital storytelling with young people. I draw on Cricket Keating's process for coalitional consciousness-building to imagine ways of addressing identity and identity-based inequities across stories and experiences. I briefly address notions of ownership and quality within community-based digital storytelling and applied theatre programs, as well as the politics (power, risk, and consequences) of practicing critically engaged performance pedagogies. I invite readers to challenge and complicate their own goals for performance practices with youth and ultimately to imagine how digital storytelling as an applied theatre practice can change the ways that artists and communities value youth in creative spaces and in society at large.

Finally, the book leaves readers with three appendices of digital storytelling and applied theatre resources. I offer an annotated bibliography of online sites and programs that address the facilitation of digital storytelling and applied theatre practices. The appendices also include a list of web-accessible digital stories created by young people in a variety of programs. I also include a list of key terms and definitions, as well as descriptions of several activities for facilitating a digital storytelling and applied theatre program with young people.

Digital storytelling presents new opportunities for situating and referencing applied performance as a tool for building alliances and enacting justice. I am interested to see how this performance work can and will transgress time, and ultimately reflect and (re)constitute the relationship between youth and society. "Thinking about the poetics of applied theatre necessitates a critical analysis of the relationships *between* all aspects of the creative process: the theatre form, its application, and its reception" (Prentki and Preston 2009: 19). As we move toward an applied theatre praxis that better reflects the twenty-first century and responds to the changing needs and desires of young people, I am excited to participate in this reimagining with an eye toward critically engaged, participatory youth media and performance practices.

The narrative of the "concerned citizen" plays in my head yet again. I am reminded once more of the possibility—the future prospect or potential—inherent in naming, performing, and seeing one's story.

Notes

1 I borrow the phrase "experience and wisdom of young people" from the mission statement of Metro Theater Company in St. Louis, MO.
2 Inside OUT was originally developed with Amanda Hashagen, Anne McNamee, and our community partners at Out Youth (Austin, TX). Anne McNamee, a former MFA student at the University of Texas at Austin in the Drama & Theatre for Youth & Communities program, was also our lead teaching artist for this pilot.
3 The Performing Justice Project was developed out of the Center for Women's and Gender Studies at the University of Texas at Austin through a grant from the Embrey Family Foundation. I partnered with Lynn Hoare and Kristen Hogan to pilot and direct this program, and the three of us continue to collaborate on the program's development, facilitation, and research agenda.
4 Here, reify means "to consider or make (an abstract idea or concept) real or concrete" (Dictionary.com).
5 Michael Anderson, John Carroll, and David Cameron's edited collection *Drama education with digital technology* (2009) includes one article on digital storytelling and drama education. Diane Conrad offers a case study of digital storytelling and applied theatre with incarcerated youth in *Youth and theatre of the oppressed* (2010). *Youth Theatre Journal* and *Research in Drama Education: The Journal of Applied Theatre and Performance* recently published special issues on digital media, each of which included new research on digital storytelling and drama. More research remains to be done.
6 Debates continue to address process versus product, as well as tensions around who is doing the applying and to whom and for what purpose. See Ackroyd (2000) and Nicholson (2005).
7 While not all applied theatre work emphasizes a self-reflective or critically conscious lens, the work discussed in this book relies on those aims.
8 The term "prosumer" was first coined by Alvin Toffler in 1981. This term is discussed in more detail in the article by Wu Qiongli (2009: 233–234).

References

Ackroyd, J. (2000) "Applied theatre: Problems and possibilities," *Applied Theatre Researcher* *1.0.* <http://www.griffith.edu.au/__data/assets/pdf_file/0004/81796/Ackroyd.pdf> (accessed March 4, 2010).

Alexandra, D. (2008) "Digital storytelling as transformative practice: Critical analysis and creative expression in the representation of migration in Ireland," *Journal of Media Practice*, 9(2): 101–112.

Alrutz, M. (2006) "A stream of conscience: Reflecting on ethics and representation in drama with youth," *Teaching Artist Journal*, 4(4): 252–256.

Anderson, M., Carroll, J., and Cameron, D. (eds.) (2009) *Drama education with digital technology*, New York: Continuum International.

Boal, A. (1979) *Theatre of the oppressed*, trans. Charles A. and Maria-Odilia Leal McBride, New York: Theatre Communications Group.

Center for Digital Storytelling. *Evolution.* <http://www.storycenter.org/timeline.html> (accessed November 11, 2011).

——History. <http://www.storycenter.org/history.html> (accessed June 3, 2011).

——home page. <http://www.storycenter.org/index1.html> (accessed November 11, 2011).

——*Stories.* <http://www.storycenter.org/stories/> (accessed June 3, 2011).

Cohen-Cruz, J. (2005) *Local acts: Community-based performance*, Piscataway, NJ: Rutgers University Press.

——(2010) *Engaging performance: Theatre as call and response*, New York: Routledge.

Conrad, D. (2010) "In search of the radical in performance: Theatre of the oppressed with incarcerated youth," in P. Duffy and E. Vettraino (eds.), *Youth and theatre of the oppressed*, New York: Palgrave Macmillan.

Dictionary.com "reify." <http://dictionary.reference.com/browse/reify?s=t> (accessed July 14, 2013).

Doyle, C. (1993) *Raising the curtains on education: Drama as a site for critical pedagogy*, Westport, CT: Bergin & Garvey.

Freire, P. (1969) *Pedagogy of the oppressed: 30th anniversary edition*, trans. M. Bergman Ramos (2006), New York: Continuum.

Goodman, S. (2003) *Teaching youth media: A critical guide to literacy, video production, and social change*, New York: Teachers College Press.

Grady, S. (2000) *Drama and diversity: A pluralistic perspective for educational drama*, Portsmouth, NH: Heinemann.

Gustavson, L. (2008) "Influencing pedagogy through the creative practices of youth," in M. L. Hill and L. Vasudevan (eds.), *Media, learning, and sites of possibility*, New York: Peter Lang.

Hartley, J. and McWilliam, K. (eds.) (2009) *Story circle: Digital storytelling around the world*, Malden, MA: Wiley-Blackwell.

Hill, M. L. and Vasudevan, L. (2008) *Media, learning, and sites of possibility*, New York: Peter Lang.

hooks, b. (1994) *Teaching to transgress: Education as the practice to freedom*, New York: Routledge.

Hull, G. A. and Katz, M. L. (2006) "Crafting an agentive self: Case studies of digital storytelling," *Research in the Teaching of English*, 41(1): 43–81.

Kershaw, B. (1992) *The politics of performance: Radical theatre as cultural intervention*, New York: Routledge.

Kincheloe, J. L. (2004) *Critical pedagogy primer*, New York: Peter Lang.

Lambert, J. (2006) *Digital storytelling: Capturing lives, creating community*, 2nd edn., Berkeley, CA: Life on the Water.

——(2009) "Where it all started: The center for digital storytelling in California," in J. Hartley and K. McWilliam (eds.), *Story circle: Digital storytelling around the world*, Malden, MA: Wiley-Blackwell, 79–90.

——(2010) *Digital storytelling: Capturing lives, creating community*, 3rd edn., Berkeley, CA: Life on the Water.

Lundby, K. (ed.) (2008) *Digital storytelling, mediatized stories*, New York: Peter Lang.

McGeoch, K. and Hughes, J. (2009) "Digital storytelling and drama: Language, image and empathy," in M. Anderson, J. Carroll, and D. Cameron (eds.), *Drama education with digital technology*, New York: Continuum, 113–128.

Neelands, J. and Goode, T. (2000) *Structuring drama work: A handbook of available forms in theatre and drama*, Cambridge: Cambridge University Press.

Nelson, B. (2011) "'I made myself': Playmaking as a pedagogy of change with urban youth," *Research in Drama Education: The Journal of Applied Theatre and Performance* 16(2): 157–172.

Nicholson, H. (2005) *Applied drama: The gift of theatre*, New York: Palgrave Macmillan.

Prendergast, M. and Saxton, J. (eds.) (2009) *Applied theatre: International case studies and challenges for practice*, Chicago, IL: Intellect.

Prentki, T. and Preston, S. (eds.) (2009) *The applied theatre reader*, New York: Routledge.

Qiongli, W. (2009) "Commercialization and digital storytelling in China," in J. Hartley and K. McWilliam (eds.), *Story circle: Digital storytelling around the world*, Malden, MA: Wiley-Blackwell, 230–244.

Rohd, M. (1998) *Theatre for community, conflict, and dialogue: The hope is vital training manual*, Portsmouth, NH: Heinemann.

Snyder-Young, D. (2011) "Rehearsals for revolution? Theatre of the oppressed, dominant discourses, and democratic tensions," *Research in Drama Education: The Journal of Applied Theatre and Performance*, 16(1): 29–45.

Taylor, P. (2003) *Applied theatre: Creating transformative encounters in the community*, Portsmouth, NH: Heinemann.

Thompson, J. (2003) *Applied theatre: Bewilderment and beyond*, New York: Peter Lang.

Vygotsky, L. (1978) "Mind in society: The development of higher psychological processes," in M. Cole, V. John-Steiner, S. Scribner, and E. Souberman (eds.), *Mind in society: The development of higher psychological processes*, Boston, MA: Harvard University Press.

Watkins, J. and Russo, A. (2009) "Beyond individual expression: Working with cultural institutions," in J. Hartley and K. McWilliam (eds.), *Story circle: Digital storytelling around the world*, Malden, MA: Wiley-Blackwell, 267–278.

Wilcox, H. (2009) "Embodied ways of knowing, pedagogies, and social justice," *Feminist Formations*, 21(1): 104–120.

Willis, P. (1998) "Notes on common culture: Towards a grounded aesthetics," *European Journal of Cultural Studies*, 1(2): 163–176.

2 Engaging the wisdom and experience of youth

In a high-rise office building at the heart of downtown, the mayor and the city's commissioners gathered in the city council chamber for a special session. As the lights dimmed, a large movie screen descended from the ceiling and the unlikely guests of these city officials, youth, and families from the Parramore neighborhood, grew quiet. A digital story narrated by several young people in the audience began to play on the screen.

> I come from Parramore
>
> I come from a place full of black people,
>
> So I identify myself as the majority

At the time of this performance, I was collaborating with three additional teaching artists and a group of youths who collectively devised and performed *We Come from Parramore*, a digital story examining their urban, US neighborhood. While the neighborhood of Parramore is sometimes touted by city officials for its "rich cultural history," the current city mayor also describes this once prospering African American district as the city's "most blighted community," citing high rates of child poverty, as well as disproportionate juvenile drop-out and arrest rates (Pathways). In 2005, city officials, non-profit organizations, and Parramore residents began significant dialogues, partnerships, and operations aimed at "reducing crime and maintaining liveable neighborhoods" in the city (National Network).

Around this same time, I had the privilege of working as an applied theatre artist for over two years with various groups of youths living and/or attending school in the Parramore neighborhood, which bordered our university campus. Together, as part of an initiative called Parramore Kidz Zone, modeled after New York's Harlem Children's Zone, we devised individual and group digital stories about a range of topics from neighborhood violence to global warming and family legacy. Within our digital storytelling and applied theatre program called Digital U, youths shared/performed some of the digital stories in public spaces, such as local community centers, churches, schools, and the city council's chamber, while other pieces played for more select groups of friends, family, and university students and faculty. Rather than measuring individual or community change specific to these performance projects, this chapter offers my experiences with digital storytelling, applied theatre, and young people; through this narrative, I explore possible frameworks and questions for facilitating digital storytelling as an applied theatre praxis, attending to how these performative practices can work to value the experience and wisdom of young people.

The Digital U: Parramore Kidz Zone project, along with the others described in this book, contributes to an ongoing debate around the relationship between youth and technology. In *Youth, Identity, and Digital Media*, editor David Buckingham warns against both exaggerating the liberating potential of intersections between youth and technology and buying into the "moral panic" around the dangers of youth interactions with new media (2008: 5). In this chapter, I acknowledge and navigate this debate by attending to somewhat utopian goals for youth-made media and performances—yes, I believe we must work from the idea that youth can and will use their creative practices to help make the kind of world they want to live in, as well as the critical challenges, such as safety and the politics of visibility, raised by live and mediated performance work with young people. Ultimately, I write about and reflect on young people and performance-making from a place of critical optimism, building on the premise that performance can and does enact possibility. Oral history scholar Della Pollock reminds her readers that

> performance is a promissory act. Not because it can only promise possible change but because it catches its participants—often by surprise—in a contract with possibility: with imagining what might be, could be, should be.
>
> (2005: 2)

Like Pollock, I argue that within and through this act of performing, and its requisite seeing and naming, we participate in possibility, in imagining and enacting potential. While risk remains inherent in this paradigm (after all, some pretty dark ends are possible),[1] more often than not, these very risks create meaningful opportunities to think about what we need/want and the complex nature of change-making.

As a teaching artist and an applied theatre practitioner, I strive to take youth creative practices seriously, as well as to work toward a just and inclusive society. Part of my job then becomes supporting young people in visioning what this kind of society looks like for them. With this chapter, I examine frameworks of digital storytelling and applied theatre as tools for preparing young people to participate in an intentional community of practice—an interactive and collaborative performance practice. I share stories of my own facilitation process as a youth-allied adult, reflecting on how critical and engaged pedagogy and performance can support efforts to value youth experiences and perspectives. Finally, I explore how digital storytelling as an applied theatre praxis, and more specifically autobiography and multimodal participation, can foster spaces for agentive selves (Hull and Katz 2006) who both participate in, and contribute to, society.

Taking youth creative practices seriously

The youth participants created *We Come from Parramore* as part of a larger project exploring the assumptions that we make about people and places. Our teaching artist team collaborated with participating young people to develop two overarching questions that framed our creative process: *Where do I come from?* and *What kind of a place do I call home?* As one of the first performance pieces devised for this project, *We Come from Parramore* served as the group's initial performative response (within Digital U) to negative media about the Parramore neighborhood, and more generally to racist and classist perceptions of minority youths living and attending school in Parramore. Throughout our creative process, the young participants who devised this digital story raised and explored questions and issues around identity and place-based stereotypes (our own and others'), as well as what it means to be part of any simultaneously real and imagined place/space defined as a neighborhood.

In the foreword to *Youth, Identity, and Digital Media*, the series editors point to digital media as a significant factor in how society views and values young people:

> While many studies of children, youth, and media have for decades stressed the status of young people as competent and full social subjects, digital media increasingly insist that we acknowledge this viewpoint. Not only must we see youth as legitimate social and political actors, but we must also recognize them as potential innovators of new media change.
>
> (Ito *et al.* 2008: ix)

In other words, digital media play a significant role in how youth and their creative practices interface with and shape society. Valerie Kinloch further suggests that the camera (and I will add formal and informal stages) offers youth an important tool for directing attention to their lives:

> Cameras of all sorts are attention givers and have the power to transform fixed understanding of identities. Whatever is receiving attention in the lens of the camera is important and requires attention; no one seems to realize this point more than the teenagers, who demand attention be paid to their lives.
>
> (2008: 54)

While paying attention to the lives of young people seems like a necessary component of valuing their lived experiences, Peggy Phelan's (1993) work on the politics and ideology of visibility offers a serious critique of this position. Building on Phelan's analysis, Deirdre Heddon points out that "visibility, *per se*, does not mean political power or equal rights" (2008: 3). Both Phelan and Heddon address visibility within performative practices such as theatre and film, offering important reminders about the limitations, challenges, and complicated power dynamics surrounding my own and other practitioners' efforts to bring attention to young people—their ideas, culture, identity, desires, etc.—even when working in alliance with young people to achieve this end. I consider Phelan's critique of visibility, even as I explore ways that applied theatre and digital storytelling might play with and disrupt the politics of youth visibility at large. I am interested in how digital and live performance practices become oppositional strategies of representation and tools for young people to exert control/agency over the quality and nature of the(ir) resulting visibility.

As a facilitator of such efforts, my own intentions to take youth creative practices seriously often include, and intentionally move beyond, goals of public visibility for youth participants and their creative work. I aim to create spaces where visibility does not equate to youth creative products becoming "worthy" of adult (specifically those in power) attention and consumption. This view merely maintains uneven and oppressive relationships between youth and their adult counterparts who seemingly exist in a more knowing, wise, or sophisticated position of authority. Instead, I focus on valuing the experience and wisdom of youth both in how I view and work with young people, as well as to what ends.

To do this, I operate from the position of what Goldman, Booker, and McDermott (2008: 202) refer to as a youth-allied adult, or a partner who understands that my own (adult) liberation is simultaneously bound with that of young people. Rather than aiming to be in charge of the youths with whom I collaborate, I strive to both acknowledge my identity-based privilege and power (e.g. my social location as a white, middle-class academic and adult) and disrupt traditionally top-down power dynamics between young people and adult program facilitators. I also participate in and facilitate creative practices that support youth in recognizing the significance of their own and each other's creative contributions, a visibility to and with themselves and each other. While attention must be paid to how performance pedagogy and practice helps build alliances with and among young people, I am focused here on what it looks like for adult facilitators to actively be in alliance with young people; after all, our view of young people and our relationship to their identity and development directly underpins how and to what end we (adult practitioners—and the likely reader of this book) facilitate performance practices with them.

In a chapter called "Introducing Identity," Buckingham (2008) offers a concise overview of many sociological and psychological perspectives around the nature of adolescence and identity, arguing that our understanding of youth identity remains largely culturally situated and continues to change. He addresses varying models of youth identity development and identification, as well as how digital media play a role in young people's concepts of self and contributions to society (2008: 2–5). Many of the models outlined by Buckingham focus on how young people "are gradually prepared, or prepare themselves, to take up their allotted roles in adult terms" (2008: 4). In my view, these models of "becoming" continue to focus on or assign value through adult-centric taste and criteria, furthering a deficit-based perspective that young people are not full social beings or subjects in their own right. Applied theatre scholar Helen Nicholson employs narrative theory to suggest that identity in general, not just adolescence or youth identity, "is a continual process of *becoming*, rather than a pre-given expression of being" (2005: 65). This view positions *becoming* as both possible and applicable to everyone, regardless of age. Thus, Nicholson's notion of becoming focuses on the ability to, possibilities for, and potential inevitability of change as a personal and lifelong asset, rather than a process of correcting deficits linked to one's younger years.

In juxtaposing these models, I am interested in moving away from binary notions of youth as already fixed, set, or complete "beings" and youth as a state of, or being in, transition, development, or "becoming." I borrow from two additional frameworks on identity to imagine a relational and socially constructed view of youth identity (a kind of lifelong becoming) that acknowledges young people as full beings in their own right. These frameworks are "identities-in-action" (Weber and Mitchell 2008: 27) and "storied selves" (Hull and Katz 2006: 44–45). Weber and Mitchell's framework for "identities-in-action" posits that youth identity can and must be considered through the lens of cultural production and activities (2008: 27). They contend that like youth's digital cultural production, "identity is multi-faceted and in flux, incorporating old and new images" (2008: 27). In other words, identity always includes elements already in existence or being, as well as new features gained through an active and cultural process of developing and interacting with the world.

Working from the notion of identities-in-action encourages arts-based practitioners to pay attention to cultural production and consumption, and specifically to how young people participate in and are shaped by such activities. Hull and Katz draw on Ochs and Capps's (1996, 2001) argument that narrative and self remain inseparable, as well as Miller *et al.*'s position that the "narrated self is a relational self" (1993: 89). Hull and Katz theorize that "storied selves ... are multiple and changing within contexts of activity and interaction" (2006: 45). Like identities-in-action, the theory of storied selves proposes that identity is context-based and can't be separated from one's activities and interactions. Hull and Katz further suggest that such activities and interactions are always underpinned by and simultaneously create narratives/stories, and thus identity/self.

Drawing on identities-in-action and storied selves, as well as tensions around being and becoming, I work from the understanding that youth identity is both individually and contextually situated, as well as part being—or already formed and in existence, and part becoming—always developing and changing in relationship to contexts, actions, experiences, and stories. Action and interaction create and build upon notions of self and identity. Identity, then, remains both set and changing, responding to and creating contexts (which we understand through story and narrative), through and in relationship to actions, context, and narrative. "Understanding that narratives can be changed ... lies at the heart of practice in applied drama" (Nicholson 2005: 63). So, within an applied theatre framework, I aim to include and respect the identities-in-action and storied selves that young people bring into the room, as well as understand that we continue to co-create new stories, relationships, and activities that foster becoming.[2]

In addition to drawing on these perspectives around identity, I rely on an asset-based perspective of young people. Rather than focusing on deficits or offering interventions to "fix" or "improve" young people, my approach to devising builds on the strengths and resources of the participants in the room. Working from a place of abundance, I collaborate with young people to acknowledge and name systemic challenges and oppressions shaping our lives, while foregrounding the positive skills, experiences, and perspectives that young people bring to specific projects and social change efforts.

In my approach to digital storytelling as an applied theatre practice, youth perspectives, then, remain integral to the work and the collaborative process. Importantly, I also acknowledge that as a trained applied theatre practitioner and as an adult, I too bring life experience and wisdom to our creative process. I cannot remove my value-laden subject position from our practice, and so I aim instead to collaborate and participate with transparency and awareness around my own perspective and privilege. By building on the assets and identities that youth bring to our creative practice, as well as acknowledging and working to disrupt traditional power dynamics between youth and adults, I work at continually *becoming* a youth-allied adult and building relationships with young people. In this role, I actively imagine and enact a world that takes youth and their performance practices seriously, a space that values intergenerational work and connections. At the core of this effort lies my belief that we all have something to gain from changing the ways that young people are viewed, valued, and engaged by society at large.

Critically engaged pedagogy and practice

We Come from Parramore resulted from eight weeks of collaborative practice, during which time we met with the young participants both in their local community center and in our technology lab at the university. Place, space, and location shaped our work processes and products, as did our focus on a critical and engaged pedagogy and performance. By intentionally considering these frameworks, our group began attending to how culture, identity, and social location, as well as reciprocity and access, played out in the logistics of our project.

We facilitated this program both in the Parramore community center, where many of the participants spent after-school time, and in the university computer lab, where several members of our teaching artist team worked and led arts and media-based programs with youth. Each site brought different assets and opportunities, as well as cultural narratives, expectations, and perspectives to our group. Week by week, we traded places, rotating at first between the two different places—located in different buildings, city blocks, and neighborhoods—and later basing our meeting place on the particular needs of our creative work at hand, as well as personal preferences of those in the room.

Not surprisingly, power functioned differently in each place and shaped how our teaching artist team and the participants negotiated their presence in each site. The community center and the university computer lab, and the people who occupied these places on a daily basis, demonstrated different relationships to young people, to ethnic and racial identities, and to our efforts to take youth creative practices seriously. Moreover, each place revealed implicit and explicit cultural codes to our group, including varying degrees of tolerance for various aspects of our project, such as young people, cameras, and justice-oriented storytelling. Negotiating project logistics in these two different places subsequently raised questions about physical, social, and cultural accessibility of place, namely this particular university campus and this particular community center, as well as how we might ensure inclusion and build trust across place-based culture and some of the resulting inequities and barriers to participation. And in some cases, our presence in each place served to confront assumptions about youth and adults associated with either the community center or the university.

Over the course of this project, our teaching artist team fostered varying degrees of inclusion and trust with and among the participants in Digital U, as well as with the staff and other non-participating members of both the university and the community center. Our interactions and experiences within the project both disrupted and created narratives associated with each place. Moreover, the project itself made visible, for both our teaching artist team and the youth participants, many of the hidden power structures operating within these given places, spaces, and locations.

Our assigned spaces—the physical room, as well as its contents and spatial arrangement—at the university and the community center also invited different levels of interaction, participation, and trust. Each space shaped how we moved and collaborated within the environment, how we shared or took ownership of the setting, and the ways that we engaged in dialogue. At the community center, for instance, we worked in a small room that included one long table surrounded by chairs. The space was familiar to all of the youths and the layout required that we sit in close proximity to one another; in my view, the room fostered intimate conversation and group dialogue, and focused our efforts to organize and storyboard our digital stories. Many of our creative writing activities, initial storytelling, and reflections on personal experiences took place in this space. Situated several city blocks away, and just outside of Parramore, the university computer lab included a large open playing space, as well as digital editing stations. The space supported theatre games and other live, physical performance activities. In addition, the access to technology in this space supported online research and digital editing of our work. Many of the youths were new to this space, which ultimately supported varying levels of comfort and types of participation. As we moved between the two places and spaces, some of the larger contexts related to location also came to bear on our creative work.

Location—a term I use to describe the social, cultural, political, and physical domains of each place and space—provided a context for our work on *We*

Come from Parramore. Everyone participating in the project literally travelled between two neighborhoods, and we all recognized the stark differences in the physical landscapes surrounding the well-resourced and heavily monitored university campus and the well-used community center tucked within a struggling city block. We also recognized blatant differences between the largely white population on the well-appointed campus and the population mostly of people of color at the underfunded community center. These differences across location, along with many others, prompted questions for our group about social location, and more specifically around the relationship between location, identity, and equity. Although certainly not new themes, identity, inclusion, and access were foregrounded in our travels from one city block to another. Questions and narratives related to the politics of place, space, and location also underpinned the youths' visual and language-based narratives that make up *We Come from Parramore.*

Within and through the politics of place, space, and location, our teaching artist team aimed to facilitate a critical and engaged pedagogy and practice. On a practical level, this meant combining applied theatre and digital storytelling to integrate critical drama-based pedagogy, traditional theatre and performance techniques, and digital media practices. Our drama-based pedagogy borrowed core tenets from critical pedagogy (Doyle 1993; Freire 1969; Kincheloe 2004), as well as liberatory, feminist, and radical pedagogies (Freire 1969; Grady 2000; hooks 1994) to focus on both individual and systemic issues of equity—both in our program and in society at large. Rather than simply working toward a highly polished digital or live and embodied performance product, we employed various aesthetic frameworks from theatre and digital media to explore the relationships between personal narrative, power, and privilege. Throughout the process, we worked to disrupt traditional hierarchies between youth participants and adult facilitators, moving away from what Freire (1969) calls the banking model of education and toward a co-constructed creative process with the youth participants. By sharing power in the room and collaborating to name and enact a process for democratic participation, we also fostered reciprocity, or mutual exchange, and began to develop shared risk-taking.

In addition, our creative process was underpinned by a strong commitment to youth engagement, from both a pedagogical and performance perspective. bell hooks's (1994) writing on transgressive pedagogy and Jan Cohen-Cruz's (2010) writing on community-based performance put forth frameworks for building dialogic and socially just practices. In *Teaching to Transgress*, hooks (1994) suggests that in addition to addressing individual and systemic oppression, engaged pedagogy specifically attends to emotion and feelings, supporting the passion, interests, and excitement of students and welcoming these often excluded forms of knowledge into spaces of teaching and learning. hooks argues for integrating the public and private lives of students, engaging personal experiences in formal learning settings, and building connections between the two (1994: 16). Cohen-Cruz (2010) similarly focuses on the centrality of individuals' lived experiences, as well as the circumstances shaping those experiences, to create what she calls engaging performance. She contends that truly engaged practices enact the notion of call and response—both responding and contributing to social questions and contexts (2010: 1).

For both hooks and Cohen-Cruz, these engaged practices—teaching and performance respectively—rely on dialogue and interaction among participating individuals. Both scholars emphasize the role of personal relationships and the need for teachers and practitioners to bring themselves fully to an engaged process. Moreover, they suggest that engaged practices require of teaching artists a willingness to express vulnerability and a commitment to one's own self-actualization (Cohen-Cruz 2010: 3; hooks 1994: 15), in addition to the well-being of their students, participants, and collaborators. Cohen-Cruz further emphasizes the importance of a professional performance aesthetic in engaged practices, suggesting that "engaged art is still art" (2010: 9). "What distinguishes engaged theatre from the mainstream is not a lack of technique … but rather the artists' actively committed relationship to the people most affected by their subject matter" (Cohen-Cruz 2010: 9).

In developing *We Come from Parramore*, we started with an interactive recruitment process focused on already existing partnerships with youths and adults in the community. Our partners at the local middle and high schools and the Department of Parks and Recreation helped advertise (by word of mouth and flyers) a meeting for young people aged 12 to 18, and invited them to learn about our evolving performance program called Digital U. Our teaching artist team also spent time in the lobby of local community centers, on the sidelines of nearby basketball courts, and in after-school homework and tutoring labs. In each of these places, we set up informal opportunities to play with digital cameras, and we dialogued with youth about the kinds of participatory and creative activities they wanted in their community. The process of laying the groundwork for participation and dialogue in this project shaped all of our work going forward; we continued to pay attention to the role of place, space, and location, as well as to how our commitment to youth-allyship and an engaged practice worked to value the experience and wisdom of the young participants.

At the official recruitment meeting, we built on these informal conversations and pitched our program proposal to a room of approximately thirty young people and a handful of youth-allied adults. We structured the pitch for participation in Digital U as an interactive process, and we invited the group to engage in theatre and digital photography exercises, view and reflect on digital stories created by youths from the neighborhood, and share their own first-person stories with the group. Drawing on elements of engaged pedagogy and practice, we wanted to demonstrate a collaborative and aesthetically framed process for creating digital stories and participating in an applied theatre practice. In this short time period, we did not expect to unpack significant social issues or questions around power and inequity. But we did hope to actively value the youths' experiences, feelings, and ideas. On paper, the interactive pitch looked something like this (see Appendix C for descriptions of the activities cited here):

Digital U: Parramore Kidz Zone Program Pitch (1.5 hours)

Preparation (40 minutes): warm-up and develop a shared vocabulary for the session
1. Break the ice with Heads Up, Heads Down.
2. Warm-up bodies and develop group dynamics with Cover the Space and Cover the Space Challenges.
3. Screen youth-created digital stories, showing pieces with different aesthetics or forms.
   a. Reflect on what stood out from the examples.
   b. Reflect on what makes a strong story.
4. Discuss content/purpose/value/experience of each activity.

Production (20 minutes): work in small groups to develop a digital postcard
5. Creative digital self-portraits
   a. Collaborative photography
      i. Capture digital self-portraits that exclude your face.
      ii. Communicate something important about yourself through the photograph.
   b. Storytelling/devising narrative text
      i. Create a line of dialogue that tells a personal story by completing the phrase "The truth about me is _____."
      ii. This "Truth about me" text becomes the photo caption for each self-portrait.
   c. Storyboarding
      i. Choose one digital image for each person in the group.
      ii. Intentionally order the chosen images and captions for an informal presentation to the full group.
   d. Aesthetic frameworks for the presentation
      i. How will your bodies, voices, and digital images hold the space?
      ii. How will you begin and end?
      iii. How will you foreground each speaker and their image?
      iv. How will you connect with the audience?

Presentation/reflection (30 minutes): share creative work with the group and reflect on connections to Digital U at large
  6. Gesture of sharing
      a. Share digital postcard drafts with the larger group.
      b. Reflect after each group presentation:
          i. What stood out to you?
          ii. Describe an image, word, or idea that felt personally relevant for you and why.
          iii. What other ideas or truths might this digital postcard suggest about young people, your neighborhood, or society at large?
  7. Reflection and closure
      a. Dialogue about how this activity represents the larger work of Digital U.
      b. Discuss logistics of participating in Digital U and invite participants to sign up.

Our commitment to serving as youth-allied adults and critically engaged/ing teaching artists manifested in how we structured the pitch, specifically with attention to youth participation, experiences, and ideas. We directed our recruitment efforts to our primary stakeholders (the young people), rather than simply the adults working with them, and increased the level of interactivity among the group as the evening progressed. The pitch started with Heads Up, Heads Down, a non-verbal theatre activity requiring relatively low-stakes participation. In addition, the outcome of this game is based largely on chance, so while it structured a reason or purpose for coming together in a circle, it did not require a lot of strategy, skill, or practice.

The embodied and improvisational elements of the activity—raising our heads on the count of three, looking directly and intentionally at someone across the circle, and not knowing if our efforts would be reciprocated—brought elements of suspense and playfulness into the room. It also brought our bodies, ourselves into the space, physically close to one another. As a participant in this game, I noticed my own demeanor shifted as I moved through several rounds of play. When I finally caught someone's eye, I engaged in a moment of recognition—the realization that I chose someone who simultaneously chose me, and that this very chance took us out of the game. I remember smiling, almost laughing out loud, in this moment of recognition; I relaxed from the act of seeing and being seen, and from my random connection to someone across the circle—even if only for a second. During this warm-up activity in our pitch, many of the participants also laughed, smiled, and relaxed a bit.

We followed Heads Up, Heads Down with Cover the Space, a non-verbal group challenge for each of us to use our bodies to cover the space—to move, walk, and stop simultaneously as individuals and as a group—all in time together. This activity required attention to individual goals of filling the space with one's body and staying evenly spread throughout the room, while remaining aware of the group and working to match slight changes in the pace of each participant's movement. With both embodied activities, we modeled the interactive and collaborative nature of Digital U, as well as our desire to simply have fun in the room together.

For the production section of our pitch, digital photography and storytelling became tools for further fostering intentional interactions with and among the youths, as well as shifting and sharing power in the room. We divided the youth participants into groups of three, giving each group a still digital camera. Relying on the youths' problem-solving skills and/or media expertise, we invited the group to use the digital cameras without a lot of explanation on operating them. Rather, we focused on the challenge of completing an aesthetic task as a collective and experimenting with the media equipment as part of that process. We asked each group to capture a non-traditional self-portrait—one for each group member. The challenge proved fairly open-ended, but included a few specific requirements to structure and support the creative process—a framework I call offering "choice within structure." Here is an overview of the guidelines we shared with the group:

> Collaborate with your group to capture a digital self-portrait of each person.
>
> Imagine how to include yourself in the image, without including your face.
>
> Communicate something that is important about you.
>
> Consider visual metaphors and creative ways to visually represent yourself.

This collective approach to digital photography foregrounded self-representation and self-reflection, while encouraging interactivity and collaboration. Each participant had to rely on their group members to achieve their desired ends. As the youths guided their peer group to capture their self-directed image, to put their ideas into action, they verbally communicated their ideas and perspectives on self—as well as their visual aesthetic—to their group members in order to achieve their desired self-portrait. While we didn't focus directly here on social questions and contexts, the youths created their self-representations in a highly social context, contributing new representations of themselves to the larger, albeit local, context of our group. And despite the adult-created and given parameters, the participants largely controlled the process of image-making; while our teaching artist team was available in a support role, the participants worked on their own and retained control of their creative process and products.

In devising lines of text for these digital postcards, the participants further reflected on their self-portraits and named things about themselves. In this familiar, but nonetheless public space, we gave each participant three to five notecards and invited them to respond in writing to the prompt "The truth about me is _____." I framed the writing process with a caveat that each participant would choose at least two of their truths to share with the group, and suggested that they carefully consider their own comfort level and the extent to which they wanted to disclose personal information. Following this individual writing time, we invited the youths to share two lines of their written text with their small group, and ultimately to work together to choose one of those lines as a caption for their digital self-portrait. At this point in the process, the participants chose which lines, which elements of themselves, to make public in our space—a decision that required analysis of and reflection on their writing, ideas, and current audience, as they made choices about how to represent themselves in our particular context.

While our framing for this activity focused simply on sharing the individual lines of text and choosing one to work with, each group took the process a step further. The youths began to contextualize their written text within their sharing process, exchanging significant moments, experiences, and stories from their lives with their group members. This process of collective sharing and exchange of personal stories reminds me that an engaged pedagogy and practice doesn't happen in the planned pitch—it happens in the margins, the in-between spaces. A critically engaged practice cannot fully take flight in a single program pitch, but the intentionality of building such practices is at the heart of this approach to digital storytelling as an applied theatre practice.

Intentional communities of practice

Tim Prentki and Sheila Preston propose that applied theatre practitioners often approach community from a constructivist point of view:

> Like sociologists, applied theatre practitioners tend to be skeptical of any tendencies towards a homogenized, essentialist concept of community and may prefer to use the theatre process itself as a form of community building, rather than starting from any preconceived idea that a given group of participants share any commonalities other than the fact of presenting themselves as participants for this process.
>
> (2009: 12)

In digital storytelling as an applied theatre practice, participants come into the work for a variety of reasons and with a plethora of identities, concerns, and passions, as well as ideas about what it means to be part of a community. Once Digital U began, we dialogued with the young people on each of these realities, working to co-construct an intentional community of practice, or what Etienne Wenger (2006) defines as a "group ... of people who share a concern or a passion for something they do and learn how to do it better as they interact regularly." Using performance itself (theatre warm-ups, storytelling, and digital media and live performance activities), we worked to build a sense of belonging.

We also created and collected theatre and media representations to explore our ideas about community. In this case, our intentionality around building a community of practice meant that we focused on choice within structure, participation and interaction, as well as experimentation and reflection. We used theatre games such as Cross the Line If … (see Appendix C) to bring individual and group concerns and passions to light, as well as to consider what it means to collaborate with an intention toward learning from one another and improving our creative practice.

Building on an ethos often underpinning applied theatre, we spent time building a deliberate process and vocabulary for working together and appreciating the contributions that each of us brought to the group. We played theatre games such as People to People (see Appendix C) and devised embodied images to explore and practice collaboration, listen and appreciate one another's voice in the room, and collectively reflect on our creative process and products. We discussed what it meant for each of us to be seen, heard, welcomed, and respected, and we agreed, both verbally and through a group contract, to hold each other accountable to a supportive, creative space. While these intentions played out to varying degrees throughout the process and for each of us in the room, our group began practicing a set of creative habits or rituals that framed our intentional community of practice and the project as a whole.

Below, I include a sample of some of the embedded practices from this project, as well as a brief outline of our overarching devising process. The repetition of key embedded practices, such as Circle Center and It Made Me Think (see Appendix C) offered us a way of ritualizing our time together. We began and ended by coming together in a circle, standing or sitting shoulder to shoulder and facing one another. At the start of each session, we engaged in some sort of "check-in" or acknowledgement of how each of us was doing—usually a non-verbal thumbs-up, thumbs-sideways, or thumbs-down to indicate how each of us felt as we entered the space, or what kind of experiences and emotions we brought to the group process. This simple act of checking in with each other, of physically sharing and witnessing statements on self, became another way of seeing and being seen, of acknowledging if not valuing one another's feelings in the room.

We also included what I call "a gesture of sharing," or moments of intentional exchange where individuals shared ideas, images, or work in progress with others in the room. These gestures of sharing were framed by intentional listening, deliberating, and reflecting back to the sharer what they saw and heard, as well as any ideas or questions to prompt improvements or help solidify creative choices. At the end of our time together, we similarly arrived back in a circle and participated in a reflective "check-out," both critically reflecting on our work of the day, and taking time to name moments, ideas, or questions that lingered. These ritualized enactments and reflections became a framework for starting to build an intentional community of practice (see Appendix C for specific examples of these practices).

Embedded Practices/Rituals

Preparation

1. Circle Center
2. Check-in
3. Embodied warm-up activities
4. Reflection

Production

5. Embodied devising activities
6. Digitally mediated devising activities
7. Gesture of sharing in pairs or small groups
8. Reflection

Presentation/reflection

9. Gesture of sharing with larger group
10. Return to Circle Center
11. Reflection with It Made Me Think

Overarching Devising Process: *We Come from Parramore:*

Preparation

1. Introduction to intentional community of practice through
   a. goals
   b. intentions
   c. activities
2. Theatre warm-ups and digitally mediated exercises focused on
   a. names, identity, interests
   b. verbal and non-verbal communication and expression
   c. collaboration and group problem solving
   d. listening, focus, sharing the space
   e. stories and storytelling

      f. embodied and mediated representation

      g. literal and metaphorical representation

      h. improvisation

      i. democratic, collective creation

  3. Introduction to digital storytelling/stories through

      a. sample digital stories

      b. digital/visual composition

      c. layers of a digital story

      d. elements and structure of story

Production

  4. Theatre and digital media devising focused on

      a. generating questions and themes

      b. individual storytelling and creative writing

      c. group text development

      d. reflection on visual metaphors and representations inspired by the text

  5. Digital media and embodied devising practice through

      a. collecting, capturing, creating digital assets (video, photos, images, sound, music)

      b. storyboarding or mapping of digital story

      c. recording of story (voice-over)

  6. Reflection on audience and purpose of story

  7. Editing of assets into digital story through

      a. rough-cut

      b. final cut

Presentation/reflection

  8. Revisiting of intended audience and purpose of story through

      a. internal audiences

      b. external audiences

      c. location of presentation

  9. Determination of framing for presentation and dialogue

  10. Performance of digital stories internally and/or externally

  11. Reflection on form, content, function of the creative work

In addition to relying on our embedded rituals, our overarching devising process included core elements from the Center for Digital Storytelling's (CDS) approach to digital storytelling. At the time of this particular project, Joe Lambert and his colleagues at the CDS worked from a set of seven digital storytelling elements[3] to help participants tap into what "makes a story a digital story, and what makes a digital story a good digital story" (2010: 9). Since that time, Lambert has moved away from the list of elements to focus on digital storytelling as a journey, or a series of steps. He revised and reordered the elements into a creative process for intentionally (and I would add reflectively) developing "meaningful digital stories" (2010: 9). Here is an outline of Lambert's (2010: 9–24) seven steps, with an abridged explanation of each action:

1. Own your insights—clarify what your story is about.
2. Own your emotions—articulate the emotional resonance of the story.
3. Find the moment—identify the moment of change in the story.
4. See your story—determine how you want your audience to see and hear the story.
5. Hear your story—find a relaxed, natural tone and pace for your voice-over.
6. Assemble your story—consider how the different layers of assets work together.
7. Share your story—determine who your audience is and what your purpose is in sharing the story. Imagine how it will get presented and framed for the audience.

While Lambert offers a process for developing personal stories, his steps also provide a map for naming and working toward notions of quality in digital storytelling.

In some ways, Lambert's steps suggest a fairly individualized and linear process for developing one's own story; however, these individualized steps can be addressed through a group process (such as a story circle, or common activities in applied theatre such as group sculpting, hot seating, vocal warm-ups, and improvisation), and many young people engage in these steps in a different order and/or simultaneously. Wenger (2006) suggests that communities of practice strive to learn from one another in order to do something better; with this goal in mind, Lambert's steps become places for evaluating, revising, and improving digital storytelling practices. Combined with applied theatre practices, Lambert's steps open up room for further intentionality around a collaborative creative process.

These three frameworks—the embedded practices/rituals that repeatedly framed our time together; the overarching devising process, which was live, embodied and digitally mediated; and Lambert's guide to creating meaningful digital stories—all supported our aims at building an intentional community of practice in different ways. The embedded theatrical rituals offered us a structured and engaging process for coming into the space, working together, and intentionally naming our commitment to a collective process. The theatre games and warm-ups also provided a hook—something playful and fun that encouraged many of us (although certainly not all of the young people) to consistently return to, and regularly interact with, the group. The overarching devising process included a focus on reflexive practice, or intentional processes for reflecting on self in relation to the group, as well as naming or marking our own learning. Moreover, we scaffolded theatre and media activities to build toward individual and group products, encouraging an intentional exchange of ideas and discoveries through the work itself and in our intentional moments of reflection. Finally, our performance-based pedagogy and practice proved cyclical and recursive; working toward an intentional community of practice, we continued to revisit what we accomplished and revise our practice based on the expressed desires of the group, as well as our shared reflections, knowledge, and questions.

The individual identities in our group also played an important role in shaping the content and framing of our creative work. While our intentional community of practice worked to value the various identities and affiliations of the participants, the community itself was not built, or dependent, on assumptions around shared identity markers or social locations. Rather, this particular community of practice was underpinned by efforts to support what James Paul Gee calls an "affinity space," or "a ... set of places where people affiliate with others based primarily on shared activities, interests, and goals, not shared race, class, culture, ethnicity, or gender" (2004: 67). We relied on youths' interest in digital media and theatre, as well as their collective focus on creating and sharing digital stories.

Poetic devising and agentive selves

Hull and Katz suggest that tensions around structure and agency, specifically, debates "over the interplay between lives as controlled and lives as having a semblance of autonomy or self-direction, has been a leitmotif of social science literature during the last half-century" (2006: 44). "Although some theoreticians find a small space for individuals to shape their life chances, the vast majority are not optimistic" (Hull and Katz 2006: 44). However, David Buckingham posits that the "alchemy between youth and digital media ... disrupts the existing set of power relations between adult authority and youth voice" (2008: ix). His argument points to opportunities within online environments for somewhat autonomous participation and possibilities for shaping one's experiences. In some ways, online engagements lack the explicit moderation of adult facilitators that typically accompanies applied theatre, as well as other school and community-based programs. In much of their online participation, youth choose their own entry points, when and how to engage, and the identities they construct and put forward in those public, albeit virtual, spaces.

As an applied theatre practitioner, I want to harness this potential for youth autonomy, while simultaneously supporting youth participation in a critically facilitated, live/embodied, and digitally mediated process. Despite the pessimistic research coming from the social sciences, Hull and Katz maintain that narrative, and more specifically the crafting of personal digital stories (and I would add applied theatre), fosters possibilities for young people to represent and enact "agentive identities," or in fact begin "to fashion identities as competent actors in the world able to influence the direction and course of their lives" (2006: 47).[4] Korina M. Jocson expands on Hull and Katz's theory to suggest that an agentive self operates as both a construct and a stance—one that invites participants "to act on transformative possibilities" (2008: 167).

Our team of teaching artists came to this project with a genuine interest in such possibilities around narrative and youth agency, specifically through the integration of applied theatre and digital media. We also wanted to explore creative approaches to learning more about young people's lived experiences and getting to the heart of what matters in their lives. To these ends, our devising process emphasized

self-representation and autobiography,

multi-modal participation,

and knowing the power of your voice.

Our focus on autobiographical stories and self-representation ultimately located youth's expertise and wisdom at the center of the project. In *Autobiography and Performance*, Deirdre Heddon reminds readers of the history of autobiography in social justice movements, such as the second-wave feminist movement: "Autobiographical performance was regarded by women as a means to reveal otherwise invisible lives, to resist marginalization and objectification and to become, instead, speaking subjects with self-agency; performance, then, as a way to bring into being a self" (2008: 3). The young people in this project similarly authored pieces of their own lived experiences, and through the creation of their digital performance pieces, they exercised some agency over how their image, stories, and perspectives were shared, performed, and to some extent viewed.[5] Through this creative process, the youths became both the subject and object of their representations, performing often hidden/invisible stories by and about US urban youths of color.

We also emphasized multimodal participation and valued multiple ways of representing knowledge and expressing self. "Youth are aware that knowledge is not neutral. They understand that some knowledge is valued over other knowledge and that certain ways of exhibiting knowledge carry more cachet than others (e.g., the privileging of printed texts over visual texts in school contexts)" (Taylor 2008: 241). This project required the creation of embodied, visual, written, oral, and audio texts and thus worked to disrupt such narrow conceptions of knowledge and ways of knowing. The youths made meaning through photography and video production, live improvisation, creative writing, embodied tableaux, voice-overs, and music, as well as the intentional, layered compositions of these varying modalities.

Lastly, we framed our devising process with an emphasis on what Maxine Greene refers to as "discovering the power of your voice" (2003: ix–x). We fostered a culture of listening and attending to the implications of our (and other's) words, stories, and images. In addition, we emphasized the act of making space for each participant to voice their point of view and be heard. Jo Tacchi, in an essay on participatory development and digital storytelling in Southeast Asia, loosely defines voice as "access to modes of expression and more generally to freedom of expression" (2009: 169). He argues that "[voice] can be about opportunity and agency to promote self-expression and advocacy, about access and the skills to use technologies and platforms for the distribution of a range of different voices" (2009: 169). With a similar view of and approach to voice, we explicitly investigated the relationship between power and responsibility in our own and other's representations, focusing on the agentive potential of basic theatre, media, and communication skills, as well as larger questions around who/what gets represented, how stories and knowledge get mediated, and who decides.

In this last section, I offer a descriptive analysis of our poetic devising process, as well as reflections on how this project aimed to engage youth as agentive selves (Hull and Katz 2006). In and through the production of their own embodied and mediatized (re)presentations, the young people in this group identified and then began complicating internal and external assumptions around their various identities. While our process and the resulting digital story continues to raise questions and challenges around representation, our devising framework aimed to value the experience and wisdom of the young participants.

Poetic Devising Framework: *We Come from Parramore*

Preparation

1. Theatre and digital media warm-ups
2. Individually respond to prompt: I come from a place …
3. Gesture of sharing
   a. Choose three responses to share with the group.
   b. Share/reflect on the responses (written and verbal text) as a group.
   c. Describe possible images and metaphorical representations of the written and verbal text.
4. Collective script development
   a. Collaborate to choose one line of text from each person.
   b. Collect, order, and edit the group's lines into a single, collaged narrative.

Production

5. Asset development
    a. Visual assets
        i. gather, create, and capture visual responses to prompt: I come from a place ...
        ii. digital photographs and video (media)
        iii. live, embodied images and gestures (theatre)
        iv. digital documentation of the live, embodied images and gestures (theatre and media)
    b. Audio assets
        i. record voice-overs of the narrative text
        ii. gather, create, and capture music and sound options
6. Storyboard of narrative text and digital images
7. Additional asset development
    a. Gather, create, and/or capture additional images as needed.
    b. Gather, create, and/or capture music and sound as needed.
8. Digital editing
    a. Develop rough-cut of digital story.
    b. Participate in a gesture of sharing.
    c. Reflect and revise.
    d. Produce a final cut of digital story.

Working from Nicholson's premise that "theatrical experiments in rewriting local stories" can begin to "dismantle ... fixed ideas of community" (2005: 90), we played with the use of poetic devising and narrative collage to create *We Come from Parramore*. While this particular digital story contains only a handful of images and lines of narrative, it was fashioned out of a larger collection of creative writings, as well as a significant focus on sharing personal narratives and reflecting on the life experiences that prompted them. The product itself represents a limited picture of the devising process as a whole.

As with our program pitch, we began with ensemble-based warm-up activities and then moved into a simple writing prompt that encouraged participants to bring hints of their lives into the room without necessarily revealing a lot of detail. I wrote "I come from a place ..."[6] on a sheet of poster paper that hung on a wall. Before inviting the youths to respond to the prompt, I improvised—loosely performed—several lines of narrative based on my own experiences:

I come from a place where no one locked their doors at night;

I come from a place where outhouses were a luxury and only cold water ran from the faucet;

I come from a place where love abounds, but sarcasm is biting, and I've learned to let most things roll off my back;

I come from a place where definitions of smart and successful are quite narrow;

I come from a place that might be ready for change;

I come from a place where young people remind me that I don't have all of the answers.

Through these performed examples, I modeled possibilities for responding to the prompt in broad and specific ways, and with attention to past, present, and future. I also used the prompt to share pieces of my own life, specifically story threads I thought could disrupt stereotypes that young people often have about teachers, professors, and artists—about me. I wanted to begin complicating ideas about visible and hidden identities, and I also wanted to demonstrate how our experiences can move into poetic bits of story. While we didn't immediately discuss any of the specifics within my lines of text, some of the participants asked me about them later in the project, and we dialogued about urban versus rural living and particular moments when we each realized that our parents are regular people. Admittedly, I worried that sharing my own lines might focus too much attention away from the young people and/or restrict the kinds of ideas the group might write about. But I also felt it was important to bring myself, including my feelings and experiences, into the room, particularly since I would continue to invite the youths to do the same. In sharing what I felt were personal and somewhat vulnerable reflections on my life, I pushed myself to take personal risks[7] in this new social space—an act that I now believe is essential to my efforts to engage with young people.

Following this example, I asked the group to consider the prompt in relation to their own lives, their own literal and metaphorical places. Working alone, the youths responded to the prompt by writing on blank notecards. They started each card with "I come from a place," adding a single thought, line, or response to the open-ended prompt. Eventually, each participant developed ten to twenty lines of autobiographical narrative, touching on where they had (and will continue to) come from at various times, moments, and places in their lives. In responding to the phrase "I come from a place," the young participants chose how to represent themselves to the group. In essence, they became the author, writer, and subject of their own narratives. Through this act of authoring, they controlled to a certain extent what pieces of themselves were named and projected in our space, as well as how they were performed and positioned—first for this internal audience, and later for an external audience. For the youths in this particular project, autobiography and self-representation became a way of naming and expressing their experiences, and ultimately producing "evidence of who they are" (Hyde 2008: 50).

Following this creative writing exercise, the youths silently read and reflected on their own notecards, choosing three lines—or story threads—to share out loud. We then moved into small groups of three or four participants and began what I describe earlier in this chapter as a gesture of sharing. They took turns reading/vocally performing their chosen lines to their group members who "listen[ed] deeply" (Lambert 2009) and with a purpose. I offered the following structure for listening and reflecting as a group:

As your peers share their story threads …

Listen deeply. Try to let go of your own story threads and focus on hearing your peers' voice and experiences.

Listen for what you see. What images (literal or metaphorical), colors, or shapes does each line of narrative evoke for you?

Listen for what you feel. What feelings or emotions does each line of narrative evoke for you?

Offer your reflections. After the speaker shares their poetic narrative, offer them a few images and feelings that each line evoked for you. Describe them in detail.

Take care of the group. Remember that each of the shared lines may be connected to important or meaningful life experiences for the speaker. Offer responses with care.

As the youths offered their reflections and aesthetic feedback, the small groups began to discuss each other's "I come from a place" lines. As in the pitch session, the youths began to discuss the larger contexts and specific stories from which their lines grew. At this stage in the process, the adults stepped back and the youths took time to pursue some of the organic conversations that ensued. They talked fairly openly with each other, sharing personal experiences and many of the full stories behind each of their story threads. In addition, many of the participants ended up sharing more than three of their lines with their small group; as one person shared a detail from their lives, another participant would offer a similar or oppositional story thread from their own pile of notecards. Without explicit adult direction/facilitation, the youths engaged with each other's experiences and drew out one another's perspectives on a variety of topics related to their lives. Conversations and connections were made across both similarities and differences.

Following these youth-led exchanges, we introduced the idea of creating a collective, poetic narrative from their individual pieces of text. In their small groups, the youths helped one another choose a single line to contribute to the collective piece. We then devised the larger narrative as a whole group. The youths physically laid out their chosen story threads on the floor—all of which started the same way ("I come from a place ...") and yet pointed to a diversity of experiences and perspectives in the group. Together, we physically ordered and wordsmithed the lines, shaped the overall structure and rhythm, and began crafting a larger, poetic narrative from the individual pieces. The youths identified through-lines and commonalities, as well as points of divergence and contrast across the poetic pieces, building an intentionally layered narrative—or picture of the places (literal, imagined, metaphorical, projected, etc.) from which they hailed. The youths moved their individual narratives (and thus elements of their personal identity) into the group's collaged (and collective) narrative. Lastly, the group worked together to develop introductory and closing lines of text that communicated something about the group as a whole. These additional lines of narrative bookended the youths' collective poem with a simple but marked shift from a focus on "I" to a focus on "we." The piece began and ended with the line "We come from Parramore."

Following the devising of their narrative script, the youths explored various layers of meaning within their narrative by devising a body of assets, or media samples, necessary for moving the script into a digital story. They returned to their small groups and again explored the prompt "I come from a place ...," only this time, they moved away from language-based text and toward multimodal explorations. Engaging through both applied theatre and digital media frameworks, the youths experimented with capturing and creating realistic and metaphorical representations of their ideas. We walked and drove with the youths through the Parramore neighborhood, where they captured their own digital photographs and video of places, buildings, people, and objects related to their prompt. We also guided the group through some physical image work (Rohd 1998: 60–67), where they improvised and sculpted tableaux (many of which were also digitally documented) of abstract ideas and feelings about place, history, and personal identity. The group also spent time researching existing images, sound effects, and music on the Internet, as well as creating their own original, collaged images in Photoshop and music in GarageBand.

Throughout our devising process, the youths negotiated the narrative, visual, embodied, and audio content for their collective performance piece. Individuals maintained final say over the representation of their original story thread, but the group primarily worked as a collective to explore representational possibilities. Specifically, they performed and reflected on each other's lines of text through physical and vocal performance choices, and collectively created and debated the digital imagery for the piece. This collaborative devising process invited the participants to negotiate decisions about how to represent themselves and their community. In performing and representing their own and each other's narratives and perspectives, they explored a variety of individual experiences in isolation and in relation to one another. Although many of the youths' assets did not end up in the final digital story, the process of devising and reflecting on them supported the participants in exploring their own identities and enacting agentive selves.

I too began to reflect on some of my own identity-markers, perspectives, and questions with the participants. With an intention toward reciprocity, I brought stories from my own life into the room and shared my personal motivations and perspectives fairly openly. Not long into our work, the youths knew that I entered this project as an applied theatre practitioner and a university professor interested in the ways that young people participate in and contribute to society through performance. They also knew that I had a lot to learn from them. As a recent transplant to the city, I was interested in how our university campus could better engage with young people in our surrounding neighborhood; the voices of our local community members were rarely present in our university classrooms. Despite Parramore's close proximity to the university campus, few relationships existed between the neighborhood residents and the university faculty, staff, and students. In moving through this project, I offered transparency around my identity, values, and beliefs. I openly named my desire to engage youth—an often marginalized population in US society—in dialogue and arts-based activism around identity-based inequities. By critically and personally engaging in our exploration of difficult topics, I participated in shifting traditional hierarchies between youth and adult facilitators. This intentionality around naming and disrupting traditional power dynamics and identity politics (the youths' and my own) permeated our process and supported our efforts to foster spaces for youth agency. These topics also played a central role in the eventual digital story itself.[8]

Below I include a descriptive storyboard, in my own words, of the youths' digital story (see Table 2.1). The descriptions outline two tracks of the group's collective digital story, specifically what you hear and what you see when viewing *We Come from Parramore*. The left-hand column includes the scripted narrative, which is performed through a recorded voice-over that includes the voices of many different young people involved in the project. The right-hand column briefly describes the digital images the audience or viewer sees in conjunction with each line of the voice-over.

Ted Rubenstein argues that "naming is a process of knowing and of agency. Once we put a name to something, we can begin to understand it and exert some agency, if not control, over it" (2005: 176). In *We Come from Parramore*, the process and product of digital storytelling operated as sites of possibility for such naming and re-visioning by youths—seeing and enacting differently—narratives about themselves and their communities. The youths experienced how their choices and their actions affected themselves and others, and ultimately shaped concrete outcomes—including our devising process, group dialogues, and performance products.

Our devising process ultimately invited the young participants to identify existing narratives about their communities and themselves. It also offered

Table 2.1 Descriptive Storyboard: *We Come from Parramore*

Transcript of the Voice-over	Description of the Visual Image(s)
I come from Parramore.	Close-up of the green street sign that reads Parramore Ave.
I come from a place full of black people, so I identify myself as the majority.	Large jar filled with black jellybeans and a sprinkling of a few brightly colored jellybeans. Circle of black people's outstretched hands warming around a small fire.
I come from a place where my family is very close, where my heart comes first, and you must dream for hope.	Image of a large family, kids with award certificates, a celebration in a house. Young man drawing a heart in the dirt with a stick. Small silhouettes of people walking on the horizon. Rays of light pouring in from the clouds above.
I come from a place where you have to have the heart of a lion to be at the top of the food chain,	Series of three images that depict big, male lions chasing, killing, and devouring an animal of prey.
where dying is not a surprise, but we still care for each other.	Desolate, rocky desert landscape. People walking past corpse of man in the foreground. Older sister in military training uniform with arm around her younger brother. Both smiling.
I come from a place where you see the police more than you see your own family,	Crowded street. Young black woman being put into police car by white police officer. Close-up of a black person's hands gripping jail cell bars.
where the lifespan is shorter than my haircut,	An EKG screen charting various vital signs; the image shows colored lines charted horizontally across a black background. Storefront of Gino's Barber Shop.
where temptation can live on your doorstep.	A white person's hands holding a red apple in front of an abstracted white torso. Close-up of scattered piles of money and little baggies of white powder.

I come from a place where money was hard to find, but love was still shared.	Boarded-up house with "Parramore" and "Keep Out" spray-painted on the front. Large group of African American youths jovially posing on the blacktop at school for the picture.
A place where kids are hungry for success,	A collage of three photos: Youth marching in the ROTC (Reserve Officer Training Corps). Youths holding a plaque/award. Youths smiling in a science lab with the governor at the table.
where going to college is like winning the lottery.	Young man walking across the stage in graduation gown with diploma in hand. Lottery tickets with two red die.
I come from a place where people are cold-hearted, because they think kindness is a weakness,	A series of three photos: Two hands shaking in solidarity. The hands begin to slip apart. The hands let go of one another.
a place where if you can't fly, you can't reach the sky.	Close-up of a crane standing in shallow still water as the golden sun rises and reflects across the water. Image of sun rising over the water and the crane flying high into the sky.
I come from a place called the bottom, so I have no other destination but the top.	Narrow, winding, rock staircase that descends into a dark, unknown place. Red winding staircase that spirals upward into a tower that reaches up and into the sky.
I come from a place, *a place,* *I come from a place called,* *a place called* *Parramore.*	A series of similar images flash on the screen: Group of youth standing on the street corner in solidarity. Arms and heads raised to the sky, toward the "Parramore Ave" sign that hangs above them.

creative, digital, and embodied structures for examining, and possibly remaking, those very narratives and identities. As a result, the product—the digital story itself—ultimately presents critiques of larger systems of power that shape the youths' lives, coupled with new ways of seeing or knowing. An early line in the digital story states, "I come from a place full of black people, so I identify myself as the majority." Two images accompany the spoken words: the first image shows a large jar full of black jellybeans and just a few brightly colored ones. The second image shows a series of hands, with outstretched fingers seemingly warming over a small fire. From all four edges of the photograph, the hands form a symmetric and aesthetically engaging, circular image of unity. By showing black people's hands together—enacting an image of self-empowered community—the story challenges assumptions about what it means to be black and/or a minority in Parramore. Black people are the majority in this neighborhood, and through words and images, the youths decenter the expected minority–majority binary that marginalizes people of color and normalizes the white majority. The renaming, reimaging, and celebrating of race-based identity markers in this digital performance interrupts oppressive narratives around black identity that are both specific to the Parramore youths and their neighborhood and contribute to larger dialogues about identity in the US.

Further using the performance of words and images to work against racist and classist assumptions about Parramore, the youths discussed what they imagined or knew other people thought about Parramore. They problematized some of those narratives, such as narrow ideas about youth support and family in their neighborhood. They performed multilayered contexts and meanings, describing the neighborhood as a place "where my family is close," where "dying is not a surprise, but we still care for each other," and "a place where money was hard to find, but love was still shared." While the story acknowledges the challenging realities of life in Parramore, the participants complicated these "expected" experiences by claiming equal importance for caring and supportive narratives of Parramore youth and families. Of their own accord, the participants juxtaposed difficult realities of poverty, drugs, and violence with narratives of an optimistic and driven generation of youth. For me, the visual and voiced narratives disrupt problematic, and yet not uncommon, perceptions about an apathetic or hopeless generation of marginalized urban youth and youth of color. Drawing on embodied and mediated representations, the youths aimed to complicate viewers' ideas about Parramore and about themselves.

While elements of this digital story work to resist identity-based assumptions and oppression, some of the narrative and visual choices also raise questions for me around the reification of identity-based stereotypes in digital storytelling. For example, a poetic line in this piece states, "You have to have the heart of a lion to be at the top of the food chain." The series of images that accompany this line of narrative show two male lions capturing, killing, and devouring another animal; the image lays out a grassy, perhaps exotic, landscape and presents a graphic depiction of the animals feeding on freshly killed prey. These images, coupled with the verbal narrative, work to dehumanize people of color by likening them to animals—a racist metaphor and meaning that troubles me as I/we work to disrupt identity-based oppression and inequities facing youth of color. Moreover, the images suggest an aggressive and violent mentality around survival in Parramore. For some of the youths, this idea of survival was a truth, a reality in their everyday lives. When I questioned the choice and meaning of these images—coming back to knowing the power of voice—the youths pushed back. The metaphor, they told me, offers an honest depiction.

As an applied theatre facilitator, I struggled—and continue to struggle—with questions around the performance of (even possibly) negative or exoticized representations of already marginalized youths. My conversation with the participants around the wild animal metaphor occurred fairly early on in our process, and I did not further challenge the youths' decision. After all, they were in agreement about the "truth" of the image, even as we explored the representation of power at play between the words, images, and context. As someone who has never lived in Parramore, I was clearly marked as an outsider to their neighborhood and to the experiences they sought to represent.

Moments such as this force me to grapple with tensions around what it means to co-construct knowledge with youth. In working toward possibilities around youth agency, I continue to negotiate sometimes competing commitments within critical and engaged pedagogies and youth participatory practices at large. Applied theatre scholar Dani Snyder-Young posits that sometimes our efforts to support youth decision-making and representational choices may in fact work to "reinforce more dominant positions than it challenges" (2011: 42). She goes on to raise relevant questions: "Where are the points of balance between honoring participants' voices and critiquing embedded assumptions? How do facilitators learn to negotiate their own authority and privileges?" (2011: 42–43). Like applied theatre work in general, digital storytelling as an applied theatre praxis raises questions about power and identity in the room (ours and the young people with whom we work), not simply in society at large. Together, these embodied and mediated practices implicate each of us in the meanings that are made and performed, disrupted and reinforced. The process and product of this digital storytelling project opened a door, if only slightly, to dialogues around these struggles, as well as my own reflections on what it means to value the experience and wisdom of young people.

By intentionally naming and representing their lived experiences (not simply accepting those created by professional media producers, city officials, or applied theatre practitioners), the youths from Parramore began to re-vision narrowly conceived ideas about their personal identity and their neighborhood. Through the production of their own narratives and performance products about their own lives, they also challenged their often assigned role as passive consumers of media culture and members of an apathetic generation. More specifically, their collective digital story offered an initial critique of discourses and systems of power shaping their lives, such as institutionalized racism, generational poverty, and state-sanctioned policing.

As with this project, digital storytelling as an applied theatre praxis offers possibilities for tapping into critical content, as well as the politics of youth participation, visibility, and agency. The theoretical and practical frameworks in this chapter begin to contend with these issues and to address how teaching artists, and society at large, might support youth agency, or their "ability to take one's place in whatever discourse is essential to action and [their] right to have one's part matter" (Heilburn 1998: 18). In his introduction to *Digital Storytelling: Capturing Lives, Creating Community*, Joe Lambert contends, "We can live better as celebrated contributors. And we can easily die from our perceived lack of significance to others, to our community and to our society" (2009: 3). With this project, we worked to foster alliances with young people and build an intentional community of practice, enact critically engaged pedagogy and performance, and support opportunities for agentive selves. Through these frameworks, we also began to actively engage and value the wisdom and experience of young people.

In a high-rise office building at the heart of downtown, a group of young people gathered with the mayor and the city's commissioners for a special session. As the lights dimmed in the chamber, a large movie screen descended from the ceiling and the city officials, an unlikely audience for the young artists' story, grew quiet. *We Come from Parramore* began to play on the screen.

Notes

1 See Ackroyd (2000) for a discussion of applied theatre and the possibility of oppressive ends.

2 Applied theatre, as a collaborative art form, raises additional questions around the relationship between individual and group identity formation. As we encourage groups of young people to work together and focus on personal interests, it brings up additional aspects of identity worthy of consideration.

3 Lambert's (2003) seven elements of digital storytelling include point of view, dramatic question, emotional content, the gift of your voice, the power of the soundtrack, economy, and pacing.

4 Hull and Katz (2006) recognize different uses of the term agency. They quote Bruner's definition of agency in psychological terms as "the initiation of relatively autonomous acts governed by our intentional states—our wishes, desires, beliefs, and expectancies" (1994: 41), as well as Freire's (1969) definition in political terms "as a belief in and the activity around remaking one's world" (Hull and Katz 2006: 73).

5 Questions arise for me around the limits of agency and choice in representation, namely if and how self-representations are always couched in others' ideas and representations of ourselves.

6 I first encountered this writing prompt in a workshop with storyteller Jon Spelman in 2002.

7 Personal risk is obviously relative to each individual and context. As a university professor and a community-based artist, the sharing of personal details with program participants crossed some of the professional boundaries I was taught to maintain. Also, I shared some details that opened up personal vulnerabilities around class and success. However, in hindsight, the material consequences of sharing these details remain relatively low risk in comparison to the privilege that I brought into the room.

8 As early as our project pitch, the youths raised questions and concerns about issues of power and inequity in their lives. While I shared my positionality and ideas openly with the youths, I remained highly aware of my power in the room and the ways that my own ideas could potentially shape, guide, and/or sway the young people's attention and intentions. Striking a balance between bringing my subject position into the room and keeping the project youth-centered is always a challenging, if not impossible, task.

References

Ackroyd, J. (2000) "Applied theatre: Problems and possibilities," *Applied Theatre Researcher* 1.0.

Bauman, R. and Briggs, C. L. (1990) "Poetics and performance as critical perspectives on language and social life," *Annual Review of Anthropology*, 19: 59–88.

Boal, A. (1979) *Theatre of the oppressed*, trans. C. A. and M. O. L. McBride, New York: Theatre Communications Group.

Bruner, J. (1994) "The remembered self," in U. Neisser and R. Fivush (eds.), *The remembering self: Construction and agency in self narrative*, Cambridge, UK: Cambridge University Press, 41–54.

Buckingham, D. (2008) "Introducing identity," in D. Buckingham (ed.), *Youth, identity, and digital media*, Cambridge: MIT Press.

Cohen-Cruz, J. (2010) *Engaging performance: Theatre as call and response*, New York: Routledge.

Doyle, C. (1993) *Raising curtains on education: Drama as a site for critical pedagogy*, Westport, CT: Bergen & Garvey.

Freire, P. (1969) *Pedagogy of the oppressed: 30th anniversary edition*, trans. M. Bergman Ramos (2006), New York: Continuum.

Gee, J. P. (2004) *Situated language and learning: A critique of traditional schooling*, New York: Routledge.

Goldman, S., Booker, A., and McDermott, M. (2008) "Mixing the digital, social, and cultural: Learning, identity, and agency in youth participation," in David Buckingham (ed.), *Youth, identity, and digital media*, Cambridge, MA: MIT Press, 185–206.

Grady, S. (2000) *Drama and diversity: A pluralistic perspective for educational drama*, Portsmouth, NH: Heinemann.

Greene, M. (2003) "Foreword" to S. Goodman, *Teaching youth media: A critical guide to literacy, video production, and social change*, New York: Teachers College Press.

Guitiérrez, K., Baquedano-López, P., and Alvarez, H. (2001) "Literacy as hybridity: Moving beyond bilingualism in urban classrooms," in M. de la Luz Reyes and J. Halcón (eds.), *The best of our children: Clinical perspectives on literacy for Latino students*, New York: Teachers College Press.

Heddon, D. (2008) *Autobiography and performance*, Basingstoke, UK: Palgrave Macmillan.

Heilbrun, C. (1998) *Writing a woman's life*, New York: Ballantyne Books.

Hesford, W. S. (2009) *Identities: Autobiographies and the politics of pedagogy*, Minneapolis, MN: University of Minnesota Press.

hooks, b. (1994) *Teaching to transgress: Education as the practice to freedom*, New York: Routledge.

Hull, G. and Katz, M. (2006) "Crafting an agentive self: Case studies of digital storytelling," *Research in the Teaching of English*, 41(1): 43–81.

Hyde, K. (2008) "Response to Wissman," in M. L. Hill and L. Vasudevan (eds.), *Media, learning, and sites of possibility*, New York: Peter Lang.

Ito, M., Davidson, C., Jenkins, H., Lee, C., Eisenberg, M., and Weiss, J. (2008) "Foreword," to D. Buckingham (ed.), *Youth, identity, and digital media*, Cambridge: MIT Press.

Jocson, K. M. (2008) "Situating the personal in digital media production," in M. L. Hill and L. Vasudevan (eds.), *Media, learning, and sites of possibility*, New York: Peter Lang.

Kincheloe, J. L. (2004) *Critical pedagogy primer*, New York: Peter Lang.

Kinloch, V. (2008) "Response to Wissman," in M. L. Hill and L. Vasudevan (eds.), *Media, learning, and sites of possibility*, New York: Peter Lang.

Lambert, J. (2002) *Digital storytelling: Capturing lives, creating community*, Berkeley CA: Life on the Water.

——(2003) *Digital storytelling cookbook and travelling companion*. Center for Digital Storytelling. <http://www.storycenter.org/cookbook.pdf> (accessed May 1, 2004).

——(2009) *Digital storytelling: Capturing lives, creating community*, 3rd edn., Berkeley, CA: Life on the Water.

——(2010) *Digital storytelling cookbook*, Digital Diner Press. <http://www.storycenter.org/storage/publications/cookbook.pdf> (accessed November 10, 2012).

Miller, P., Hoogstra, L., Mintz, J., Fung, H., and Williams, K. (1993) "Troubles in the garden and how they get resolved: A young child's transformation of his favourite story," in C. A. Nelson (ed.), *Memory and affect in development: Minnesota symposium on child psychology*, 26: 87–114, Hillsdale, NJ: Erlbaum.

National Network on Preventing Crime in the Black Community resources page: "Orlando's Parramore neighborhood: A case study in preventing crime in the black community," <http://www.preventblackcrime.com/pcbc.nsf/5a5f27b419c03e618525797d0057065e/b2fc94e813fe07418525797d0054812a?OpenDocument> (accessed March 18, 2012).

Nicholson, H. (2005) *Applied drama: The gift of theatre*, New York: Palgrave Macmillan.

Ochs, E. and Capps, L. (1996) "Narrating the self," *Annual Review of Anthropology*, 25: 19–43.

——(2001) "Living narrative: Creating lives in everyday storytelling," Cambridge, MA: Harvard University Press.

Pathways for Parramore: "Pathways for Parramore leads revitalization efforts for Parramore heritage district," City of Orlando, Florida website. <http://www.cityoforlando.net/elected/parramore/index.htm> (accessed July 2011).

Phelan, P. (1993) *Unmarked: The politics of performance*, London: Routledge.

Pollock, D. (ed.) (2005) *Remembering: Oral history performance*, New York: Palgrave Macmillan.

Prentki, T. and Preston, S. (eds.) (2009) *The applied theatre reader*, New York: Routledge.

Rohd, M. (1998) *Theatre for community, conflict and dialogue*, Portsmouth, NH: Heinemann.

Rubenstein, T. I. (2005) "Taming the beast: The use of drama therapy in the treatment of children with obsessive-compulsive disorder," in A. M. Weber and C. Haen (eds.), *Clinical applications of drama therapy in child and adolescent treatment*, New York: Routledge.

Shawyer, S. (2012) "Review of *Engaging performance: Theatre as call and response*," *Theatre Topics*, 22(1): 103–104.

Snyder-Young, D. (2011) "Rehearsals for revolution? Theatre of the oppressed, dominant discourses, and democratic tensions," *Research in Drama Education: The Journal of Applied Theatre and Performance*, 16(1): 29–45.

Tacchi, J. (2009) "Finding a voice: Participatory development in Southeast Asia," in J. Hartley and K. McWilliam (eds.), *Storycircle: Digital storytelling around the world*, Malden, MA: Wiley-Blackwell.

Taylor, I. D. (2008) "Response to Pleasants," in M. L. Hill and L. Vasudevan (eds.), *Media, learning, and sites of possibility*, New York: Peter Lang.

Weber, S. and Mitchell, C. (2008) "Imaging, keyboarding, and posting identities: Young people and new media technologies," in D. Buckingham (ed.), *Youth, identity, and digital media*, Cambridge: MIT Press.

Wenger, E. (2006) "Communities of practice: A brief introduction." <http://www.ewenger.com/theory/> (accessed January 3, 2013).

3 Building knowledge about self, others, and society

Just outside of Phoenix, AZ, on the Gila River Indian Community, a young man captures and informally narrates video of a gorgeous farming landscape that helps feed his community; this landscape was once the site of a Japanese internment camp. His digital story, which includes some of this footage, illuminates many questions around systemic, racial violence both past and present. In Austin, TX, a young person writes a story about coming to understand how their own gender identity has been largely constructed—by family, friends, society, and capitalism. His digital story offers insight around transgender identities, as well as how words and images shape our beliefs about ourselves and what seems possible. In Orlando, FL, a young woman devises a digital story about attending a life-changing church camp and escaping neighborhood violence. Her digital story raises significant questions about how class, culture, and religion shape our perspectives on life. Like *We Come from Parramore*, these digital stories each reflect the wisdom and experience of young people. They draw the viewer in through compelling perspectives and offer both direct and somewhat incomplete narratives that leave room for audiences to make their own meaning. They also demonstrate how personal stories can connect to a wide range of audiences as they raise larger questions related to identity, knowledge, and power.

Stories, both personal experiences and the larger metanarratives that underpin them, help us make sense of the world around us and shape the ways that we participate in public and private areas of society. This chapter explores how preparing and performing digital stories provides opportunities for young people, as well as those who work with them, to build knowledge. Within digital storytelling as an applied theatre practice, young people embody ideas, crystallize their perspectives, and consider how their lives exist as part of larger contexts. In a study on youth theatre and personal and social development, Jenny Hughes and Karen Wilson argue that "exploring the world through a creative process widens young people's frame of reference and provides new perspectives and knowledge about themselves, the community and the wider world" (2004: 65). In my experience, the process of devising theatre and media supports the exploration of personal stories to widen or deepen these frames and reference points. Young people express and represent their experiences through the use of body and voice, as well as photography, video, and music. Drawing on metaphors, symbols, and emotions, they aesthetically communicate their feelings and experiences—often in ways that are new to them or provide new ways of thinking about their lives or a given topic. They literally see their stories—themselves—in images and on-screen, next to other people's stories, and thus a part of narratives that exist beyond themselves.

In Chapter 2, I examined the creation of group narratives, for which each participant contributed at least one poetic line of dialogue and one image to a short, collective performance piece. Through this creative group process, I focused on valuing the stories and experiences of young people in the room. With this chapter, I explore the creation of more traditional digital stories— two- to three-minute digital performance pieces that feature a single personal narrative. Like the collective digital storytelling process outlined in the previous chapter, I approach the devising of individual stories as a collaborative, as well as aesthetically and critically engaged, process. Participants may respond to a writing prompt on their own, but they soon work collaboratively to develop one of their stories more fully and to communicate a question, journey, or narrative arc. The participants' individual digital stories are later collected in one place, such as a DVD or an external hard drive, if not strung (digitally edited) together as intentionally sequenced scenes.

Despite my focus on developing a full digital story by and about each of the participants, applied theatre situates digital storytelling as a social, relational, and interactive process. The participants share their identities and experiences with each other, encountering new stories and forms of knowledge that are often ignored, marginalized, or kept out of spaces designed for young people. I believe that seeing and responding to each other's work, as well as performing each other's stories, supports young people in framing or reframing their past and present, as well as generating ideas about themselves and their future. The relationships between the young participants, as well as among and between their individual performance pieces, create exciting opportunities for reflecting on and creating knowledge.

Social and relational practices

Several years ago, I signed up to attend a three-day digital storytelling work-shop led by the Center for Digital Storytelling (CDS). Before I arrived, the staff at the CDS emailed me a thorough packet of information on digital storytelling, including some concrete guidelines and strategies for developing a draft of my personal story and gathering old family photos or other images to visually represent my narrative. Much of the groundwork for developing my digital story took place before I arrived at the workshop or met anyone else in our group. I brainstormed stories from my past, drafted a rough narrative for two of them, and collected existing photographs that seemed to relate to the time period or content of my stories. While this process proved rather efficient (I created a quality digital story in three days!), I struggled with a couple of key elements. I was not able to find personal or family photos that supported these stories from my past (as a child, my family didn't own a camera) or reflected the point of view I now hold on these narratives.

Admittedly, I was not used to planning or devising stories without a team of voices at the table with me. I kept imagining ways to explore my stories with an ensemble or a community of practice that could help me discover new ideas, images, or meanings in my experiences. I felt certain that with a group of collaborators, I could capture some exciting photos in the old house where the digital storytelling workshop took place. Also, despite a wonderful story circle on the first day of the workshop, I wanted to know more about the people in the room. I wanted to explore their stories and listen to the significant life moments that shaped their perspectives on these experiences. The workshop turned out to be an awesome experience; still, by the end, I longed for the embodied and ensemble-based process that remains so central to applied theatre.

In "This Is What I See: (Re)envisioning Photography as a Social Practice," Kelly K. Wissman theorizes young women's participation in a long-term, collaborative photography and poetry writing workshop called "Sistas!" (2008: 13–45). She draws on conceptualizations of literacy as a social practice to propose that photography—a way of seeing, understanding, and communicating—is also a form of knowing and socially constructing meaning. Literacy, or the ability to see and understand, is often dependent on social and cultural access to meanings and contexts. In this way, knowledge and meaning is socially constructed. Wissman critiques standard photography instruction for its primary focus on skill acquisition (2008: 39), arguing that "envisioning photography as a social practice recognizes that the images produced are not simply a transparent recording of reality; rather, the images encapsulate a particular framing of that reality that is highly intentional and unique" (2008: 14). Viewing photographers (in this case, the young women in her workshops) as "social beings with historical legacies, emergent identities, and social commitments" informs how and what images are produced, as well as how they are interpreted and received (2008: 14).

With this intentionality toward socially situated photography, and thus literacy, Wissman aimed to cultivate an anti-racist and feminist context for the young participants to creatively express what they know about themselves and the world around them. The stories, images, and experiences of the participants became the primary texts of the workshop. Moreover, Wissman focused on the "primacy of relationships in fostering knowledge production" (2008: 40). She used photography to demonstrate the importance of social practices in the making of meaning and understanding of self. Reflecting on the participants' photography, Wissman observed that the young women understood how identity shapes meaning. "The students' images emerged from lived experiences and reflected an awareness of how social identities matter in taking photographs and in constructing knowledge about experiences" (2008: 40).

My approach to applied theatre similarly emphasizes social and relational practices as a vehicle for developing and creating performance work and building knowledge. Groups of young people work as an ensemble to create and perform their own and each other's stories. Embodied images, movement sequences, and narratives are explored in and through social and relational interactions. This kind of socially engaged devising process promotes possibilities for interpersonal connections between young people. Moreover, applied theatre emphasizes not only social relationships between people but also relationships among ideas, experiences, and images.

Working within an intentional community of practice where the participants share their lives through performance can change the experience and purpose of telling our stories. In the *Digital Storytelling Cookbook*, Lambert points out that how we tell our stories depends on the audience:

> When we hear stories, we listen for answers that we can relate to our own lives. Honoring self-narratives through creative expression with an audience in mind, even an audience of one, offers the opportunity to not only record and string together your insights, but change how others think and feel ... What you are trying to say, and how you say it, depends on who is listening, what they already know and don't know, and what you want them to know. What may be a story intended solely for you may end up being a story that changes someone else's thoughts or feelings. And conversely, what may be a story for someone else may end up changing the way you think or feel.
>
> (2010: 10)

James Thompson goes further to suggest that "every moment of performance, and particularly the public acts or displays of a group's theatrical work, actively creates 'webs of significance' between people" (1999: 70). These initial connections to a story or a performance can prompt a desire to know and relate to other people. In this way, social and relational practices create conditions for the possibility of belonging or intimacy with others.

For Aimee Carrillo Rowe, "the sites of our belonging constitute how we see the world, what we value, who we are becoming" (Rowe 2009: 3). Rowe's writing on feminist alliances and democratic subjectivity theorizes the politics and limitations of relations and belonging. She argues that our sense of belonging both grows out of and constitutes our experiences with and understandings of the world:

> Broader socio-cultural forces intertwine with intimate forces to provide maps of meaning through which we come to comprehend experience. At every level of the movement among experience, consciousness, and agency, belonging is a constitutive force. The conditions giving rise to experience, the maps of meaning through which we come to make sense of experience, and the possible strategies we may imagine or deploy to intervene in those conditions are all generated within our sites of belonging.
>
> (2009: 4)

Borrowing an example from Ruth Frankenberg (1996), Rowe further demonstrates how the nature or qualities of our social and relational practices—not simply that we engage in them—also prove influential in our ability and desire to work in and toward alliances:

> [A] white woman is more likely to gain experiential access to racism and, in turn, to gain consciousness and cultivate resistive strategies to racism's conditions when she cultivates intimate ties with people of color (Frankenberg 1996). The range of options available to the subject—for experience, interpretation, and in turn agency—arise out of the specific collectivities into which we insert ourselves or are inserted.
>
> (2009: 4)

In my reading of Rowe (2009), she emphasizes how relationships with people across difference can develop opportunities for increased understanding and thus agency or action. Sites of belonging, or spaces of intimacy, arise across the intersections of our identities and experiences. At the risk of stating the obvious, belonging, then, operates as a key factor in our desire and ability to develop relations across "power lines" (Rowe 2008)—the systems of power, oppression, and unearned privilege that separate us unless we work against them—and in turn to begin tackling identity-based inequities.

Admittedly, though, belonging is not a given result of the facilitation of social and relational practices. In her book *Power Lines: On the Subject of Feminist Alliances*, Rowe (2008) expands on the limits of relational practices and the challenges of building alliances across complex systems of power. Relational practices and building alliances require reflexivity and a willingness to be vulnerable with one another. They also necessitate a willingness to examine one's own unearned privilege, as well as one's own complicity in oppressive systems that might underpin personal values or experiences. The practice of becoming an ally or working in alliance requires addressing difficult realities, questions, and risks related to the intersections of identity, power, and justice. The difficulties of this practice become especially poignant in work with and for young people, and in sites such as schools and other state agencies, which rely on the maintenance of often hegemonic ideologies. Unfortunately, theatre with and for young people often attempts to ignore realities of racism, sexism, and homophobia. In avoiding these struggles in work with youth, we cannot hope to build real alliances, or sustained belonging, with each other—with young people.

Stories as knowledge and perspective

Drawing on Elizabeth Ellsworth's theories on critical pedagogy and knowledge, Mia Perry asserts that "devised theatre can provide the space for 'knowledge in the making'" (2011: 63; Ellsworth 2005: 4). In other words, as an ensemble creates images, scenes, and stories, they simultaneously explore, disrupt, and make meaning. Moreover, devising relies on participants' experiences and interests as primary sources of knowledge for creating performances. In applied theatre settings, participants' stories offer entry points for looking at individual and systemic issues of power through the already familiar lens of personal experience. By considering those lived experiences through an aesthetic lens, such as photography, video, embodied movement or tableaux, young people make the familiar strange and begin to examine and see their experiences in different ways. In addition, aesthetic representations of abstract concepts or ideas such as injustice can become accessible by taking on the appearance of a real or concrete image or object, such as representing systemic racism with the image of black hands gripping jail bars. In the personal narrative that follows, a young storyteller reflects on the painful relationship between gender–justice and self–acceptance, as well as the liberation that can come with knowing how you fit—or belong—in the world. The devising process for this digital story both drew on and created layers of knowledge; it fostered awareness, perspective, and understanding within the storyteller and, I would argue, within our ensemble as a whole.

Not a Bird or a Plane

For most of my life, I felt like I was floating on a breeze. But now I am grounded on a rock in clear air. Today, I know who I am. I was taught as a child my future was to be a wife and a mother. I can remember many times growing up when my cousin imagined our dream weddings, when my mother told me what it would be like to raise my kids, when my friends and brothers reinforced that I was a girl and therefore different from them. They painted a vivid picture. I could never see where I was supposed to fit into it, but I didn't know how to do anything but play along. Having been forced into a mold I couldn't fit into made growing up confusing, some-times even heart-rending. I'd have surges of anger and denial about my body that no one had patience for. I struggled to find a role for myself around peers driven by crushes, lust, romantic drama—things that I some-how had to think were important too. Such a foggy sense of self-identity, I couldn't see my hand or future in front of my face. By the time I headed for college, I spent most of my time with my friend the Internet. Aimless web surfing one typical day landed me on a website called AVEN (Asexual Visibility & Education Network), a forum where I found a group of people bonding over their mutual love of cake, and not sex. They called it asexu-ality. Such a simple idea, and yet for me it caused a paradigm shift. There is nothing so intensely satisfying as making sense of your self at long last. The Avenites were the most diverse group of people I had ever met, and among them were people who identified as about 38 more flavors of gender than I had ever known existed. I loved that they existed, that none of them had settled for stuffing themselves into the boxes that society put them in— that I didn't have to fit myself into my pre-made box. I decided that I identified as androgynous, leaning female almost immediately. And it was like a running start down a steep slope. I noticed the way other people interacted with me, the assumptions they made about me because of my gender, and I realized how wrong that felt. I looked at my body for the first time in a long time and remembered with new intensity how much I hated it. I spent months and months examining my memories and personality, making sense of things that always seemed out of place, pulling myself apart, and piecing together a truer, stronger identity. Now, at the end of that journey, I know who I am: an asexual, trans man. My struggle has not ended, but at last, I can take strength in a newfound identity and a future to look forward to. Today I am standing on a mountain in clear air, grounded in myself and focused on the path going straight up.

This narrative grew out of a digital storytelling program called Inside OUT. Over the course of nine months, I co-directed this performance project with teaching artists Amanda Hashagen and Anne McNamee at a local center for lesbian, gay, bisexual, transgender, queer, and questioning youth, as well as their allies. After several months, our group consisted of a small, core group of young people, several youth-allied volunteers, and a handful of other young people and staff who played with us intermittently, contributing to group performance pieces and supporting the core team's development of individual digital stories. Just as in the Digital U program, we used theatre and performance pedagogies, as well as digital media examples and activities, as tools for reflecting on personal experiences. We engaged those same tools to envision how personal experiences, when aesthetically performed and shared, might illuminate important ideas for our internal group, as well as for an outside audience. While not all of the stories created in Inside OUT chronicle such a specific journey around identity, each storyteller touched on aspects of personal identity and how their experiences ultimately shape their beliefs about themselves, others, or society.

Our devising process relied heavily on sharing personal stories: first, to help us get to know one another and build an intentional community of practice; then, to actively value the experiences and perspectives of the people in the room; and later, to imagine how our personal experiences offer unique forms of knowledge and possibilities for social change. Writing and aesthetically representing stories presented what I call "moments of knowing," or times where a common understanding develops, or new ideas come to light within the creative process. While everyone's creative process was somewhat unique, we all brought personal experiences and perspectives to the group. We explored those experiences through aesthetic forms that were not always familiar to participants, such as theatre-based image work and photography. In addition, we facilitated the work through a critical lens on identity and oppression. Here, I include an outline of the practical frameworks that we used to devise individual digital stories in this program, focusing again on preparation, production, and performance.

Devising Frameworks: Producing Individual Digital Stories

Preparation

1. Theatre and digital media warm-ups for building skills and intentional community
2. Review three layers of a digital story
   a. Vocal track: voice-over of the narrative
   b. Visual track: photos, video, transitions, titles, words, special effects
   c. Soundtrack: music and sound effects
3. Individual script development
   a. Generative storytelling with the ensemble
      i.   The Truth about Me
      ii. Digital Self Portraits
      iii. Improvised Story Circles
      iv. Story prompts, such as "A time when …"
      v.   Branches of Significance
      vi. Timed Storytelling Activities
      vii. Draw your place, space, location with details.
   b. Script and story writing
      i.   Fill up a notecard.
      ii. Fill out an "I am poem."
      iii. Respond to an open-ended prompt in writing.
      iv. Poetry writing
   c. Gesture of sharing
      i.   Share your story narrative with a partner or small group.
      ii. Analyze your story using the Center for Digital Story-telling's seven steps.
      iii. Gather ideas for possible images and metaphorical representations of the written and verbal text.
      iv. Respond to and critique stories by
           • creating three frozen images with your bodies;
           • creating captions or titles; and/or
           • sharing what you see when hearing the narrative.
      v.   Group reflection and deliberation over creative choices and additional options

    d. Script development and revision

        i. Personal reflection and deliberation on group feedback

        ii. Develop and solidify written narrative

Production

4. Asset development

    a. Visual assets

        i. Group and individual reflection and deliberation on the emotional and visual landscape of your narrative

        ii. Gather, create, and capture visual representations of that landscape through

- digital photographs and video (media)
- live, embodied images and gestures (theatre)
- digital documentation of the live, embodied images and gestures (theatre and media)
- digital editing or collaging to create new images

    b. Audio assets

        i. Group and individual reflection and deliberation on the emotional and auditory landscapes evoked by your narrative.

        ii. Perform and audio record voice-over of personal story.

        iii. Gather, create, and capture music and sound options.

        iv. Edit voice-over, music, and sound layers of your story.

5. Storyboarding narrative text and digital images[1]

6. Gesture of sharing

    a. Pitch storyboard and explain aesthetic choices.

    b. Give and receive feedback.

    c. Deliberate over potential assets and pathways for moving forward.

7. Additional asset development

    a. Gather, create, and/or capture additional images as needed.

    b. Gather, create, and/or capture music and sound as needed.

8. Digital editing

    a. Rough-cut of digital story

    b. Gesture of sharing

    c. Reflection, deliberation, and revisions

    d. Final cut of digital story

9. Dramaturgy
   a. Archive and edit multiple digital stories together for a viewing.

Presentation/reflection

10. Gesture of sharing
    a. Share internally with community of practice.
    b. Share externally with invited audience.

Through these kinds of practical and pedagogical frameworks, we facilitated the transformation of memories and stories into visual and audio performances. We also guided the youths through an intentional process for constructing new knowledge, beginning from their own lived experiences and moving toward aesthetic representations (see Figure 3.1).

Starting with personal stories allowed us to ground the creative process in the participants' familiar experiences, and thus locate the youths in the role of experts. To gather personal stories, we began with reflective memory work, guiding the youths through a series of interactive theatre and identity-based activities to generate story themes.[2] We also facilitated structured and free-form writing sessions[3] to help the group recall significant moments from their lives and to experiment with narrative storytelling. The youths engaged in prompt-based photography,[4] drawing,[5] movement,[6] and sensory recall activities to bring

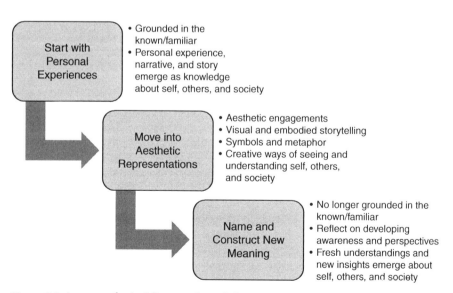

Figure 3.1 A process for building new knowledge.

additional details of their memories to the forefront of their minds. Helen Nicholson argues, "One of the social functions of memory is to contribute to shaping the future by providing people with insights into the past and by offering symbolic frameworks through which to interpret contemporary experiences" (2009: 269). Through these aesthetically engaged activities, the youths articulated personal memories and experiences, and ultimately considered their lives through past-, present-, and future-oriented narratives: What did these experiences mean at the time they occurred, what do they mean now, and what do they offer me for the future?

In line with Nicholson's theories on memory, Knut Lundby asserts that such narratives operate as cultural tools, revealing modes of thought and providing vehicles of meaning-making (2009: 185). Like the youth in Wissman's "Sistas!" workshop, these young participants' personal narratives demonstrated their particular ways of thinking and knowing. Their narratives also became the primary source of knowledge or material from which we made meaning in the room together. In addition to revealing truths, facts, feelings, and perspectives held *by* members of the group and *about* members of the group, the stories themselves offered unique perspectives on culture and society.

In *Performance Affect: Applied Theatre and the End of Effect*, James Thompson cautions against a performance practice focused only on meaning-making in a cognitive or narrative sense. Pointing to Peggy Phelan's (1997: 17) argument around the limitations of "interpreting encounters with bodies," Thompson observes that

> by working solely in the realm of effect where performance communicates messages or concentrates on identifiable social or educational impact, the practice becomes restricted or weakened. By failing to recognize affect— bodily responses, sensations and aesthetic pleasure—much of the power of performance can be missed.
>
> (2009: 7)

While I agree with the premise put forward by Phelan and then Thompson, I remain conscious of how bodily responses and aesthetic pleasure in and of themselves contain and produce such messages. Internalizing these meanings can result both in concrete knowledge and ways of knowing that are innately connected to social, if not educational, contexts and impacts. In helping young people bridge these mind–body (cognitive and affective) connections, and in working to expand what counts as and constitutes knowledge, digital storytelling as an applied theatre practice can attend to both effect and affect.

After exploring memories and significant moments in their lives, each participant in Inside OUT chose one of their experiences or a series of related moments to present as a digital story. In addition to creating a narrative or script, they began to represent and share their story through an aesthetic lens. We used many of the same theatrical and media-based activities from our memory work, including oral storytelling, photography, and creative writing, as well as embodied images/tableaux, gesture work, and music, but at this stage we focused on developing a chosen story, rather than unpacking our memory banks and digging up possible story threads. In moving toward aesthetic representations of a single story, the group considered how to communicate a particular piece of their lives through visual symbols and metaphors. They eventually paired each of the big ideas or beats from their narrative with an aesthetic asset, namely a still photo or a short video clip.

Applied theatre relies on these kinds of aesthetic explorations to help move participants beyond their everyday or ordinary experiences and perspectives. While traditional theatre often creates fictional worlds that bridge to real life, this approach to digital storytelling employs digital images, performance, and sound to create symbolic and metaphorical representations of inner feelings and non-fictional worlds. Audrey Thompson, who theorizes around anti-racist pedagogy, argues that "[art] takes up where we are, but at the same time shifts us, introducing us into new and surprising relations. No longer grounded in the familiar, we begin to construct fresh understandings, and in the process, reconstruct ourselves" (1997: 32). In this case, the creator of *Not a Bird or a Plane* attended to a series of familiar experiences that marked his early years. During our memory work, he recalled several moments where he did not fit in or that he failed to meet other people's gendered expectations. In beginning to visually represent these moments through embodied statues, photographs, drawings, and Play-Doh sculptures, he tapped into how seemingly benign interactions with family and friends repeatedly provided him with narrow and often wounding messages about identity and self-worth. This idea eventually became the crux of his narrative and then his digital story.

Toward the end of our devising process, members of the ensemble organized a field trip to a local toy store to capture assets for their digital stories. In videotaping and photographing aisles of toys, the youths realized that the store largely organized the products by color and stereotypically gendered content: pink versus blue aisles of toys and separate areas for female dolls and largely male and androgynous action figures. The photographs from this excursion visually communicated many of the painful divisions and highly gendered messages that this young participant internalized throughout his youth: *girls must desire, if not embody, pink princesses, while boys must personify action figures and superheroes.* In Table 3.1, I include my own narrative storyboard outlining the combination of voiced narrative and visual aesthetics performed in *Not a Bird or a Plane.*

This aesthetic exploration, and the resulting concrete and realistic images, underscored his experiences with gender biases in a significant way, prompting the young participant to revise lines of his narrative. He rewrote small sections of his story, explicitly naming how seemingly harmless assumptions around identity were tied to his own frustration and rage as a young child and a teenager. He combined a serious and calm voice-over with a series of fast and playful video clips and photographs from the toy store, highlighting the confusing and highly gendered nature of his upbringing. Moreover, he communicated some of the

Table 3.1 Descriptive Storyboard: Not a Bird or a Plane

Transcript of the Voice-over	Description of the Visual Image(s)
For most of my life, I felt like I was floating on a breeze. But now I am grounded on a rock in clear air. Today, I know who I am.	Video clip of a blue sky with puffy white clouds. An action figure of Superman, held by a hand, slowly crosses the sky from left to right. Title scrolls across the bottom of the screen: *Not a Bird or a Plane.*
I was taught as a child my future was to be a wife and a mother.	Video camera pans a series of activity books from the 1950s. The covers show girls in pink dresses and boys in blue sweaters and ties. The titles of the books read *Friendship Bracelets, Learning to Sew, Things to Make,* and *Let's Get Crafting.*
I can remember many times growing up when my cousin imagined our dream weddings,	Video camera pans an aisle of stacked pink boxes with small dolls in princess dresses.
when my mother told me what it would be like to raise my kids,	A colorful mural of kids playing in a green field beneath a blue sky and a bright rainbow.
when my friends and brothers reinforced that I was a girl	A bike rack filled with children's bikes; Pastel pink bikes are lined up on one side and pastel blue bikes are lined up on the other side.
and therefore different from them.	A bike rack filled with blue and red bikes; a red lawn mower sits besides the bikes.
They painted a vivid picture. I could never see where I was supposed to fit into it, but I didn't know how to do anything but play along.	Video clip of the storyteller rolling out black Play-Doh and using a blue cookie-cutter of a "girl" to create a figure.
Having been forced into a mold I couldn't fit into made growing up confusing, sometimes even heart-rending.	A Rubik's cube—all blue squares are lined up and face the viewer. A hand turns the cube to reveal a white side, then a red side, and finally a green side of the perfectly organized cube.
I'd have surges of anger and denial about my body that no one had patience for.	Video clip, over the shoulder of the storyteller, who looks into a bathroom mirror. He sprays a foggy foam over the mirror, distorting his reflection in the mirror.

Narration	Visual
I struggled to find a role for myself around peers driven by crushes, lust, romantic drama—	Slightly out-of-focus images of books titled *The Act of Kissing* and *Lost Love*, as well as romance novels with men holding passed-out or swooning women.
things that I somehow had to think were important too.	A shelf of comic-book toys, lunch boxes, and accessories. The focus of the image is a box that reads "Obsessed with MARVEL."
Such a foggy sense of self-identity, I couldn't see my hand or future in front of my face.	A repeat of the image of the fogged-up bathroom mirror that only slightly reveals the reflection of a person.
By the time I headed for college, I spent most of my time with my friend the Internet.	An image of a shadow box dressed up to represent a drive-in movie set. Tons of boxcars are lined up at the drive-in.
Aimless web surfing one typical day landed me on a website called AVEN (Asexual Visibility & Education Network), a forum where I found a group of people bonding over their mutual love of cake, and not sex.	Video clip of the storyteller's hands at a computer keyboard. The camera pans to the screen which displays the home page for AVEN. The viewer sees the mouse arrow click on "enter forum."
They called it asexuality.	The camera pans a bolded definition of asexuality on the website.
Such a simple idea and yet for me it caused a paradigm shift.	An image of a Rubik's cube with all of the colored squares scrambled on all sides.
There is nothing so intensely satisfying as making sense of your self at long last.	Fast-motion video clip of hands putting together a puzzle. The clip ends with a completed picture of a dinosaur.
The Avenites were the most diverse group of people I had ever met,	An image of a boxed toy set of bendable Gumby and Friends figures. The figures are a variety of shapes and colors.
and among them were people who identified as about 38 more flavors of gender than I had ever known existed.	Camera pans a shelf filled with a wide variety of action figures in different shapes, colors, sizes, and materials. None of the figures are in boxes.
I loved that they existed,	Images from a toy store, including a picture of Rosie the Riveter with the words "We can do it!" and a box of moustache bandages.

(continued)

Table 3.1 Descriptive Storyboard: Not a Bird or a Plane (continued)

Transcript of the Voice-over	Description of the Visual Image(s)
that none of them had settled for stuffing themselves into the boxes that society put them in—	Camera pans a shelf of Lego figures, each individually boxed for sale.
that I didn't have to fit myself into my pre-made box.	Images of products from a toy store, including a shopping bag that reads "As lovely as Aphrodite and as wise as Athena," a poster of Kent Clark ripping open his shirt to reveal his Superman suit, and Hello Kitty dolls dressed in costumes of other characters from the same line of toys.
I decided that I identified as androgynous, leaning female almost immediately.	Hand-drawn sign, written in a pale purple and black marker, that reads "Androgynous."
And it was like a running start down a steep slope.	Image of Superman, Robin, and Batman flying downward toward a cityscape.
I noticed the way other people interacted with me,	A small patch of wild flowers blowing in the wind.
the assumptions they made about me because of my gender,	A store-bought bouquet of brightly colored flowers, followed by an image of a large, plush stuffed unicorn surrounded by other stuffed animals.
and I realized how wrong that felt.	Pink Hello Kitty products on a toy store shelf.
I looked at my body for the first time in a long time and remembered with new intensity how much I hated it.	Two hands are manipulating a Play-Doh, cookie cutout of a girl. The hands erase the details of the cookie-cutter girl, and only the outline of the figure remains.
I spent months and months examining my memories and personality,	Handmade sign that reads "Gender Fluid." The letters alternate pink, green, blue, and purple.
making sense of things that always seemed out of place,	A fast-motion video clip of a mixed-up Rubik's cube being turned to reveal each of its sides.

Narration	Visual
pulling myself apart, and piecing together	A fast-motion video clip of the completed dinosaur puzzle getting pulled apart.
a truer, stronger identity.	A handmade sign that reads "male" and is written in black marker. On top of the period after the word "male" sits a stick figure with short hair, glasses, and a flower in his hand.
Now, at the end of that journey, I know who I am: an asexual, trans man.	An image of a blue sky with white puffy clouds. Photograph from the Phoenix Comicon featuring the storyteller in a Superman T-shirt next to Leonard Nimoy, who played Spock in the original *Star Trek* series.
My struggle has not ended,	Video clip of the storyteller sitting on the floor with a pile of mixed-up puzzle pieces in front of him. He mixes them around and then sits back and takes the pile in.
but at last, I can take strength in a newfound identity	Return to the image of Clark Kent ripping open his shirt to reveal his Superman suit.
and a future to look forward to.	Photograph of the Out Youth logo painted in large letters across the side of a garage.
Today I am standing on a mountain in clear air, grounded in myself and focused on the path going straight up.	Return to the video clip of a blue sky with white puffy clouds. A hand flies an action figure of Superman up through the sky and toward the clouds. The figure moves from screen left to the middle of the screen and the picture fades out.

highly gendered marketing strategies bombarding children. The completed digital story demonstrates the role of family, friends, and society in fostering ideas around gender and ultimately limiting young people's understanding of gender identity and themselves.

According to Mallika Henry, "Symbols have been widely recognized as media for assigning meaning and using that meaning to communicate publicly—to culturally educate. Drama, through its use of symbols, has been a powerful tool for communicating public and political meaning" (2000: 58). The images and symbols in *Not a Bird or a Plane* communicated an often-accepted cultural expectation around gender identity. Exploring his personal story through an aesthetic lens helped this particular participant make "sense of things that always seemed out of place," namely his experiences of living on the border of hegemonic, or standardized and oppressive gender norms. He critically engaged with visual and embodied images to reflect on already familiar experiences, such as playing with cousins and listening to his mother's expectations about becoming a parent. And in this process, he formed new perspectives and named new insights about himself, his family, and society at large. As Henry notes, drama is perspectival and "in all learning, *wider and deeper* perspectives are the hallmarks of wisdom and knowledge" (1999: 252). This story ends with a playful video clip of a handheld action figure of Superman flying through a perfectly blue sky. *Not a Bird or a Plane* reveals a sense of freedom and stability (at least in the moment) for the storyteller that came with developing or deepening his knowledge and perspectives on self and society.

In addition to fresh perspectives for the storyteller, this aesthetically engaged process offered the Inside OUT ensemble opportunities for examining how everyday, normalized activities and experiences relate to systemic issues of oppression and injustice. Lee Anne Bell references Green (2004) and Roberts (2005) to argue that "aesthetic engagements help us envision new possibilities for challenging and changing oppressive circumstances" (2010: 17). In other words, visual symbols and creative explorations offer opportunities for seeing possibilities. Images and aesthetic engagements can move feelings and not-yet experienced ideas into more concrete, visible, or imaginable forms. In turn, metaphorical and abstract images can help communicate the emotional content of our lived stories and experiences in a way that goes beyond traditional narrative communication.

The devising of *Not a Bird or a Plane* cultivated some of these occasions for the storyteller, our ensemble, and audience members who viewed the piece. This story itself also produced a counter-narrative to the many gender-biased experiences and representations that can and do go unnoticed or critiqued by youth and adults alike. Our aesthetic engagements prompted group discussions around individual and systemic oppression, including the role of language, images, and marketing in maintaining hegemonic norms. The young storyteller reflected on the oppressive role that identity-based biases, specifically sexism, played in his own life. Within his story, he also named how experiencing other people's stories created a paradigm shift around his understanding of self, gender, and sexuality.

Furthermore, the ensemble tapped into how we, along with our friends and family, sometimes participate in narratives and social systems that perpetuate stereotypes and other oppressive ideas around gender identity. Working as an intentional community of practice, the group developed new understandings about self, others, and society—providing necessary groundwork for young people and youth-allied adults to begin challenging identity-based oppressions.

Making meaning about self, others, and society

Through storytelling and image-making, the young participants in Inside OUT transformed elements of their lived experiences into concrete knowledge— namely, ideas about themselves and ways of seeing, perceiving, and under- standing experiences, facts, and other people. Our process began with intentions and opportunities to represent and reflect on self. As with *Not a Bird or a Plane*, the participants' stories, when coupled with live and mediated performance work, became catalysts for reflecting on much more. Table 3.2 outlines some general understandings about self, others, and society often developed by young people within digital storytelling as an applied theatre practice.

While in many ways young people are experts on their own lives, they often begin to see themselves as such through the process of creating and sharing digital stories. Digital storytelling as an applied theatre practice creates spaces for articulating knowledge and deepening not just what we know but also how we know it.

In my own work, I witness young people realize, often for the first time, that their stories matter to other people and are worth telling. I see them realize how their stories relate to other people and events in ways they had not imagined. In *Not a Bird or a Plane*, the storyteller suggests that his perception of himself significantly shifted when encountering other people's stories on the Internet— both about gender identity and sexuality. Experiencing how others' stories impact our own lives, which often happens in applied theatre, can change the ways we value and understand the power of our own stories. Moreover, parti- cipating in this aesthetic practice helps create and solidify knowledge of who we are and what matters to us.

In *Storytelling for Social Justice*, Lee Anne Bell asserts that "stories operate on individual and collective levels," bridging personal experiences with those of a particular group or society at large (2010: 16). For the creative ensemble in Inside OUT, this process of bridging between self and others often resulted from careful deliberation, both individually and as a group. Creating digital stories provided opportunities to question seemingly neutral experiences—such as encountering children's toys—and to think about how narratives reflect and perpetuate systems of power, as well as underpin indi- vidual and collective identities. By intentionally representing their own knowledge and understandings of the world, participants gained conscious- ness around how metanarratives, or the stories we live by, wield power and shape what each of us values.

Table 3.2 Making Meaning Around Self, Others, and Society

Making Meaning About:	Understandings Developed:
Self	My stories and experiences are worth telling.
	My stories and experiences are a form of knowledge.
	My stories and experiences represent, produce, and contribute to knowledge in society.
	My stories and experiences are related to my identities.
	My view of others is shaped by my own identities, experiences, and stories.
	My knowledge about myself is developed in social and relational practices.
	Differences, similarities, and incompatibilities with others can offer knowledge about myself.
Others	Others' stories and experiences are worth knowing.
	Others' stories and experiences are a form of knowledge.
	Others' stories and experiences represent, produce, and contribute to knowledge in society.
	Others' stories and experiences are related to their identities.
	Others' view of themselves and of me is shaped by their own identities, experiences, and stories.
	Others' knowledge about themselves and about me is developed in social and relational practices.
	Differences, similarities, and incompatibilities with others can offer knowledge about other people.
Society	Our stories and experiences are part of a larger set of narratives.
	Our stories and experiences are shaped by local and global systems and histories.
	Our stories and experiences are often the result of and contribute to systems of power.
	Our stories and experiences can reveal dominant and hidden discourses in society.
	Our stories and experiences can help envision and enact changes we want to see in the world.

Weber and Mitchell rightly warn that "reflexive regard is not necessarily critical—it is still situated in and shaped by culture and experience" (2008: 41). While self-reflection and perception cannot be wholly separated from our culture or experiences, applied theatre helps young people notice the power-laden relationships between self and society. The creative process invites ensemble members to reflect on themselves and the implications of their held perspectives. Youth then participate in intentional deliberation, bringing their reflexive regard to the group setting where they share ideas and listen to others' perspectives. In these deliberations, they often encounter differences in experience and knowledge, if not beliefs. Etchells (1999) contends that in some ways this kind of discord proves essential to the devising process. In writing about his work as the artistic director of Forced Entertainment, he contends, "This does not result in an ideal democracy or consensus building expertise; in fact, the differences between the collaborators are often depended upon in the creative process … Collaboration was never about perfect unity but about difference, collisions, incompatibilities" (1999: 56).

For many youth, devising remains one of the few activities or spaces that model how to simultaneously debate ideas and value difference. Through this process of critical deliberation, or informed decision-making, young people learn to see how self and others, self and society remain intertwined. In creating digital stories through a social justice lens, young people also realize (dis)connections between their personal (such as home-based) and public (such as school-based) experiences. For example, the participants in Inside OUT listened to a variety of viewpoints, analyzed their own experiences, debated ideas, and made mindful choices about how to represent their own truths. As they "crystallize[d] meanings into concrete images" (Neelands and Goode 1990: 19), they took ownership of their knowledge and presented personal perspectives for a public audience. While each story certainly includes unexamined ideas and narratives, many of the youths produced critically conscious stories that explicitly value difference and work to counter oppressive or hegemonic norms and narratives.

By the last few weeks of Inside OUT, each member of the ensemble participated in the creation of several if not all of the digital stories performed and produced by the group. The youths shared rough-cuts of their digital stories and helped each other capture and create last-minute images, sound, and music to complete their stories. Using performance-based tools and reflection techniques,[7] they conjectured and deliberated on the messages, feelings, and other meanings that each story might leave with viewers. At this stage, the participants also articulated through lines and dissonant perspectives presented across their collection of stories, such as the importance of family approval and how state laws surrounding birth certificates and parental rights shape gender bias.

We built on this discussion and created an intentional line-up for the digital stories. The line-up mapped out how the stories would be archived together on a DVD and an order for playing the stories at a semi-public screening. The archival and dramaturgical process of imagining the pieces together invited the group to consider how the collection of digital stories might communicate new meanings, feelings, or political ideas. Bringing the stories together into a single archive also raised questions about representation and required the group to seek what Mallika Henry calls a kind of synthesis or "coherence in the multiple voices while acknowledging a script" (2000: 51). In analyzing the texts as a single script or viewing the pieces as a single performance, what new narrative arc(s) or questions arise? How might the stories critically engage some of our common belief systems? How does the emotional landscape of the performance shift with different choices around the order of the stories, such as beginning or ending with a particular story?

With these questions in mind, the ensemble deliberated over how to effectively title their collection of pieces—a choice needed to simultaneously represent individual stories and the collection as a whole. The eventual title, "One Second at a Time," was heavily debated and revealed the participants' individual and personal stake in the process of collective representation. How do we maintain our individual identities while becoming part of a group or collective? How do we value differences in the stories and across identities within an effort toward cohesion? While their stories were vastly different in form and function, the group's eventual title communicated the youths' shared desire to practice patience with themselves and others, while aiming to make change in the world. Arriving at this shared vision, or title, was an exercise in building understanding and knowledge about the relationships among the stories and the storytellers.

We understand the world and our place in it through the stories and events that we see, hear, and experience. The Storytelling Project and other programs that explore first-person stories and oral histories serve as reminders that "stories carry common sense" (Bell 2010: 16). Unfortunately, this "common sense" too often includes racist, sexist, and otherwise oppressive, and yet normalized, narratives. Mia Perry writes about contemporary performance practices with youth, further asserting that the process of devising new work or stories "illuminates grand narratives and dominant discourses," many of which are masked as this kind of common sense (2011: 70). As the Inside OUT ensemble viewed their collection of stories in succession and discussed the larger contexts of the stories themselves, patterns of identity-based inequities and systemic oppression faced by members of the ensemble came to light or gained emphasis in new ways. The participants recognized repeated themes in the visual and narrative discourses, such as feelings of alienation and vulnerability, as well as a lack of acceptance by family or finding the strength to accept one's self when society does not. In reflecting on their digital stories, they articulated how their own narratives and desires, including aspirations around marriage, equality, or the desire for "2.2 kids and a white picket fence," can be implicit and complicit within hegemonic, racist, classist, and otherwise oppressive social narratives. They also recognized how image and story can be used to disrupt and remake their relationship to these narratives. Participating in digital storytelling as an applied theatre practice exposed not only how stories and experiences carry vestiges of systemic oppression and perpetuate dominant discourses in society but also how stories can envision and enact ideas we want to see in the world.

Double Diamond design process model

Throughout the Inside OUT project, moments of knowing developed out of individual and group deliberations. The Design Council, a UK-based non-profit focused on harnessing the transformative power of design thinking, outlines a practical approach to the creative process called the Double Diamond design process model (Hunter "What Design"). I find their model useful for developing and structuring spaces for deliberation throughout digital storytelling and applied theatre work with youth. The Design Council's model (see Figure 3.2) grows out of research on solving design-related problems and illustrates a four-step process of divergent and convergent thinking. The visual symbol of the double diamond represents an iterative process for engaging in action and reflection toward specific goals. Designers develop creative ideas and products by expanding their knowledge base and then thoughtfully narrowing down possibilities before developing a prototype.

As a teaching artist, I am particularly interested in the model's attention to research, analysis, and repetition. In my own work with youths, participants often move through a two-step process of gathering ideas (preparation) and moving them directly into an outcome (production), essentially going through just one of the diamonds in this model, often without much attention to analysis or deliberation. Sometimes this process is dictated by time restrictions, but more often than not, it results from a focus on arriving at the product instead of moving through and valuing the creative development process. In contrast, the Double Diamond design process model process suggests additional stages of deliberation that include a more refined practice of divergent and convergent thinking. In moving through all four phases of the Design Council's

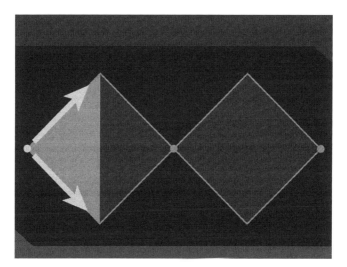

Figure 3.2 Double Diamond design process model (Resources for Learning 2012, adapted from the Design Council 2005).

model, youth repeatedly gather ideas and expand their frames of reference. They also refine their thinking and move toward deeply considered creative solutions. This repetition and its inherent spaces for deliberation remain crucial to building and deepening knowledge. The process also reflects an emphasis on exploring possibilities, not simply landing on a product.

Mat Hunter, Chief Design Officer at the Design Council, refers to the first step of their model as the *discover phase* (Hunter "What Design"). Using a process of divergent thinking, designers expand their knowledge and experience by broadly collecting ideas related to a topic or problem. In other words, they engage in a research and brainstorm process to gather knowledge about a particular idea or question. In my approach to digital storytelling, the *discover phase* invites youth to share several of their own stories, learn about the experiences of others, and gather new stories and perspectives through interviews, theatre and media-based memory work, and more traditional research.

This *discovery phase* is then followed by the *define phase*, a process that requires convergent thinking, or a critically engaged process of analyzing, assessing, and narrowing down their collected ideas. In this step, young participants evaluate the viability of those ideas and participate in deliberations that help narrow possibilities or directions for further exploration. The focus on letting ideas go and taking time to define a project's direction guides participants to reflect on and scrutinize the materials they gathered. In this phase of digital storytelling, young people share and listen to multiple stories before deciding on a topic or experience to address in their digital story. This might happen through a story circle, timed storytelling activities,[8] or drawing exercises such as Branches of Significance[9]—all of which generate and expand ideas and resources. It also means gathering and exploring a variety of potential assets, such as digital images or music, before choosing an aesthetic for their digital story.

Young people participate in multiple gestures of sharing and deliberations that are focused on divergent and convergent thinking. They offer and receive critiques, questions, and suggestions for honing in on potential story threads and viable concepts for developing a product. During these deliberations, they begin listening and relating their own lives to various perspectives from within the ensemble. As part of this first diamond, participants weigh a variety of creative choices within the group setting and hone in on one or two options for further exploration and development.

Moving into the second diamond of the Design Council's model, young people practice divergent thinking once again. The second diamond begins with the *develop phase* in which participants expand and deepen their thinking, only this time with a more targeted and in-depth focus on their most viable idea(s) established during the *discover* and *define phases*. For example, young people might explore different ways to articulate a specific experience from their lives. They could experiment with different narrative forms, styles, or voices, as well as how and where to name their own point of view within the story. Moreover, they might try out possible opening lines for their story, or explore tone of voice or visual aesthetics to reach a particular audience. In general, the *develop phase* offers an opportunity to play with possibilities for representing a particular story, theme, or idea.

The final stage in the Double Diamond model is the *deliver phase*. Through another process of convergent thinking, designers deliberate over project details and implement a final product. In my approach to digital storytelling, youth assess their representational options for viability,[10] as well as meaning and impact. After carefully weighing their gathered options, they choose a course of action, storyboard their plan, and implement their chosen ideas into a digital performance piece. Executing ideas within this phase also relies on deliberation and, in some ways, the double diamond process occurs again within this last phase. For example, when editing a digital story, participants finally see their chosen images in place while listening to a voice-over. Despite planning and prior reflection, this experience of seeing the pieces of a digital story together often yields additional decisions, and a new opportunity for narrowing or honing in on representational solutions. Furthermore, the Design Council's four phases constitute a regenerative cycle of praxis. The *deliver phase* gives way to a larger process of reflection on the project as a whole. After building and sharing digital stories, youth participants often gather additional reflections and feedback on their process and products to inform future projects, and, in an ideal situation, these ideas get refined and archived for application in future projects.

Moving beyond traditional design work and problem solving, I engage the Double Diamond design process model to support a critically engaged creative process. The four phases, particularly the transitional moments or turning points between divergent and convergent thinking, require engaged deliberation. As young people shift from gathering ideas to narrowing ideas, from deepening ideas to producing ideas, they have to make choices that require analysis and deliberation over concepts, points of view, and aesthetics. This process invariably impacts their perspectives. The youth first examine who they are and how their stories operate as knowledge. Moving from personal stories to aesthetic representations, they engage in several stages of interpretation, drawing on what they already know to begin filling in gaps of experience or understanding that arise in the creative process. They also explore and perform point of view—both theirs and others—by recalling and interpreting a narrative, capturing digital images, and performing a voice-over. The ensemble then considers how their stories, experiences, and ideas are similar and different from others, as well as how they relate to larger social issues and questions.

Within this process young people see and interpret how their experiences count as knowledge and relate to their sense of belonging in the world. They examine what personal stories suggest about society and its underlying value systems. Moreover, they explore how power is reinforced or disrupted by stories and personal experiences. In this way, the Double Diamond design process model offers teaching artists and young people a replicable process for deliberation, and thus the development of critically conscious creative products.

Possibilities for knowledge and belonging

I approach digital storytelling and applied theatre with the belief that we all benefit from seeing how our identity matters and understanding that identity and power are concepts worthy of attention. In examining identity and power with young people, I strive to cultivate what bell hooks calls radical openness, or "the will to explore different perspectives and change one's mind as new information is presented" (2003: 48). The will to learn from another's stories or experiences and change one's point of view based on new knowledge underpins possibilities for experiencing belonging as well as becoming an ally or engaging the struggle for social change. hooks (1990) suggests, and I agree, that the practice of freedom in education requires opportunities to take in, conceptualize, and improvise alternative realities in our lives. In my view, imagining a just world becomes possible when we see and understand each other's personal experiences as valuable and consequential forms of knowledge or truth.

Based on her own digital storytelling work with youth, Korina Jocson asserts that "what begins as a personal project turns into a highly social activity where language, race, class, gender, and experience merge, a place for imagining selves, constructing texts, acquiring new literacies, and evoking possibilities for change" (2008: 171). If knowledge about self, others, and society creates opportunities for imagining new worlds and working across identities, then capturing and sharing what we know, including our personal stories and experiential knowledge, proves essential to creating a more just society. Furthermore, disrupting identity-based inequities such as racism, classism, and sexism necessitates a collective desire to examine our collective knowledge and ways of knowing, as well as our own identities and related power lines, for their respective biases.

Digital storytelling as an applied theatre practice enacts inquiry about the world and our place in it. Through this inquiry, I see participants develop a triple consciousness of sorts, gaining awareness of their relations, or the connections between themselves, others, and society. As I mention in Chapter 2, digital storytelling invites youth to see themselves both perform and performed on-screen; they are at once the subject and the object of the inquiry and the performance. Participants also gain a sense of self through the eyes of another. In addition to seeing themselves reflected in and through the stories, images, and interpretations presented by other ensemble members, and playing themselves within their own and others' stories, youth see how they (self) exist in relation to others. This work can also move young people beyond the experience of a self–other dichotomy; as connections and understandings develop between people, lines between self and other blur or become valued differences rather than boundaries. These multiple and layered ways of seeing and knowing prove representative (looking back) and constitutive (looking forward), reflective and actively engaged in understanding that which has already occurred or is currently occurring and imagining that which doesn't yet exist.

While not without challenges or limitations, critically engaged performance work can reveal systemic oppressions based in race, ethnicity, gender identity, sexuality, class, and/or dis/ability. Talal Asad argues that "pain is not a private experience, but a public relationship" (2003: 81). Through the sharing of emotionally evocative experiences, some of these relationships become visible. In *Not a Bird or a Plane*, the storyteller addressed his experiences with injustice related to gender identity and sexual orientation—ideas not often represented in public spaces or the popular media. While he shared a personal and individual story, he aesthetically (visually and emotionally) represented his experiences through images common to a fairly general public, if not accessible to people across a variety of social locations. Witnesses to this digital story shared their own connections to *Not a Bird or a Plane*, revealing an array of struggles with injustice related to identity markers both similar and different to those addressed in the story. Viewers articulated connections between this story and ways that class and religion (two ideas not directly addressed in the digital story) shaped their own beliefs about fulfilling gendered expectations and personal happiness. Other viewers expressed newly gained knowledge about sexuality and new understandings around the social–emotional challenges facing transgender youth. The story's themes of identity-based oppression inspired deliberations among our ensemble members and then invited audience members to consider often hidden and systemic forms of oppression. Moments of knowing and hints of belonging materialized across these spaces as well. Each of these moments emerged from within a group of individuals already largely familiar with struggles and experiences facing the LGBTQ community, and yet new knowledge, dialogues, and personal connections still emerged from creating and sharing this digital story.

Developing vocabulary and consciousness around identity-based oppressions, however, does not always result directly in alliances, meaningful relations, or anti-racist or liberatory performance work. Rowe reminds me that

> relationality arises neither from obligation nor fetishization, but from a yearning for one another that is expressed through holding ourselves accountable to our intersecting, divergent, and power laden histories and moving from there. It is a labor of love that takes place in compassionate conversation, historical investigation, and relational excavation.
>
> (2009: 5)

Building meaningful relations across power lines—across and about identity and difference—requires an uncoerced desire for accountability to each other. To this end, Rowe calls for "bridge-work," or the taking of "responsibility for the engaging, the need to become fluent in each other's histories" (2009: 5). Sharing and listening deeply to each other's stories creates conditions for this very fluency to develop. In my experience, building knowledge of one's self and others, as well as how power functions in and through one another's bodies, language, and actions, makes living and acting in alliance imaginable. Knowing someone's story helps build connections and accountability to their experiences.

In Chapter 2, I wrote about adults working in alliance with youth (youth-allied adults) to create spaces that value the experience and wisdom of young people. Here, I extend this discussion to the necessity and possibility of building justice-oriented alliances among youths. Lee Anne Bell asserts that social justice allies work toward a "vision of society in which the distribution of resources is equitable and all members are physically and psychologically safe and secure" (1997: 3). Aiming for this ideal, allies engage in the struggle to address not only the ills that grow out of social injustice but also the systems that create and perpetuate them. Paolo Freire's (1969) recognized theories on literacy suggests that knowledge of and access to language reveals how power functions and underpins our ability to engage in the struggle for justice. Within our digital storytelling work, youth come to know what they know, articulating places, spaces, and systems of power in their own lives. Moreover, they recognize their own spaces of privilege as they begin to examine the social locations and identities at play in the ensemble's stories. When given an opportunity to examine their own experiences with privilege and oppression next to larger social narratives and concerns, they often begin to understand how the oppression of individuals perpetuates larger systems of inequity that hinder possibilities for everyone and anyone to live in a just society. This relational understanding—specifically around the connections between self and other, self and society—comes in part from working with other youths and connecting to experiences different from their own. But it also comes from critical engagements around how power functions through narrative. This awareness around the power of language, coupled with a sense of relationality and the will to critically examine their lives, creates the conditions necessary for working in alliance and across differences (hooks 2003; Rowe 2009).

I remain cautious, though, about the liberatory possibilities of newly fostered relations within digital storytelling or applied theatre work; actively engaged alliances move beyond representational and dialogic practices in the struggle for justice. While digital storytelling as an applied theatre practice does not always create or sustain youth alliances, knowing and understanding the stories of other people remains a necessary component for cultivating belonging, or agency and accountability, among others. In my own practice, this very sense of belonging has proven critical for fostering radical openness and alliances among young people. As Rowe observes, "The work, then, is to learn to represent ourselves in relation to one another" (2009: 6)—a well-matched challenge for applied theatre practitioners and youth alike.

Toward new knowledge

Digital storytelling as an applied theatre practice operates as a creative and generative process, not simply an exercise of memory recall. Through personal storytelling and critically engaged performance-making, participants reflect on and explore their lives and perspectives. They choose what is significant to them and about them, as well as what parts of their identity to share with others. Ultimately, they share a deliberated point of view for a public of some sort.

As an applied theatre practice, digital storytelling attends to youth's experiences as meaningful knowledge that reflects the past and shapes the future.

My approach to digital storytelling locates youth and their personal narratives in relational contexts. As a critically engaged and relational praxis, this approach speaks to Watkins and Russo's (2009) concerns about the insular nature of most interactive technologies. Through critical reflections on self, others, and society, young people gain opportunities to share and create knowledge in dialogue with societal questions and debates. In this way, digital storytelling begins to blur the line between public and private knowledge. The work invites youth participants and audiences to think and feel deeply about how our lives are shaped by and perpetuate stories and narratives of truth. Finally, young people engaged in this creative practice experience the relationship between performer and viewer, or producer and consumer. With attention to how and why images and narratives are created and consumed, young participants act as critically engaged prosumers, producing the very narratives they desire to see and consume.

James Thompson cautions against grand success narratives in applied practices, observing that "the impressive results within the group-work room often are not translated to 'gains' on the outside" (2003: 70). Rowe (2009) echoes Thompson's caution around utopian claims for social change in her writing on alliances. However, she goes on to suggest that we have much to gain from looking at the very places where alliances do not materialize:

> Sometimes the space between subjects does not open into alliance. Sometimes we turn away from difference. The point here is not to find fault in such moments of failure, but rather to turn toward such moments, to see what we can learn from turning. Sometimes we turn toward one another, sometimes we turn away.
>
> (2009: 8)

So while I rarely have the opportunity to research if or how this work results in lasting alliances among youth or larger goals around social change, I know that something important happens in and through this creative process. Youth's stories and knowledge become visible to themselves and others. Moreover, their narratives contribute to a picture—a vision—of the world and possibilities for alternatives ways of living and being. Youth participants experience and analyze the production of knowledge—how truths get constructed, maintained, and disrupted by both individuals and systems.

Not a bird and not a plane. What will we see, know, and create next?

Notes

1 Storyboarding can be completed at various stages in the project, including early on as a tool for brainstorming assets, in the middle of the process as a tool for

organizing and assessing assets, or near the end as a map for editing final assets together.

2 See activities such as The Truth about Me, Cross the Line If …, and Complete the Image. Descriptions for many of these activities can be found in Appendix C.

3 See Lambert (2002), Lee Anne Bell (2010), and Jan Cohen-Cruz (2010) for examples.

4 Prompt-based photography was a devising technique in which we gave participants a prompt, such as "I wish people in my life paid more attention to things like …" Youth would then respond to the prompt by taking a digital photograph, rather than writing, telling, or physically embodying their ideas.

5 For example, we used a guided narrative to prompt participants to draw minute details of their bedroom or a safe place where they spent a lot of time. Recalling and drawing these details on paper brought up many memories and stories of the space and time.

6 We used guided pantomimes and choreographed gestures of repetitive activities from our lives to aesthetically explore everyday tasks and ideas that we often embody without much thought.

7 Specifically, we used Liz Lerman's Critical Response Process (Lerman and Borstel 2003), a method for gaining feedback on creative work, as well as techniques such as DAR (describe, analyze, reflect/relate), It Made Me Think, and Writing in Role. Descriptions for several of these activities can be found in Appendix C.

8 Timed partner activities might include telling a story to a partner over the course of two minutes, changing partners and telling the same story in one minute, changing partners again and synthesizing the story into 30 seconds, and finally sharing the essence of the same story with a new partner in a matter of 10 seconds or six words.

9 Branches of Significance is a drawing activity that invites participants to visually map out five to ten of the most significant crossroads, or moments of decision or change, in their lives. These "branches" on a timeline of people's lives often point to thematic or experiential possibilities for a digital story narrative.

10 In this context, viability refers not only to how narrative works toward intended goals but also to how feasible it is to capture desired images, music, or sound.

References

Asad, T. (2003) *Formations of the secular: Christianity, Islam, modernity*, Stanford, CA: Stanford University Press.

Bell, L. A. (1997) "Theoretical foundations for social justice education," in M. Adams and L. A. Bell (eds.), *Teaching for diversity and social justice: A sourcebook*, New York: Routledge.

——(2010) *Storytelling for social justice: Connecting narrative and the arts in anti-racist teaching*, New York: Routledge.

Bell, L. A. and Griffin, P. (eds.) (1997) *Teaching for diversity and social justice: A sourcebook*, New York: Routledge.

Cohen-Cruz, J. (2010) *Engaging performance: Theatre as call and response*, New York: Routledge.

Design Council, "About us." <http://www.designcouncil.org.uk/about-us/> (accessed March 5, 2013).

Edwards, K. E. (2006) "Aspiring social justice ally identity development: A conceptual model," *NASPA Journal*, 43(4): 39–60.

Ellsworth, E. (2005) *Places of learning: Media architecture pedagogy*, New York: Routledge.

Etchells, T. (1999) *Certain fragments: Contemporary performance and forced entertainment*, London: Routledge.

Frankenberg, R. (1996) "When we are capable of stopping, we begin to see: Being white, seeing whiteness," in B. Thompson and S. Tyagi (eds.), *Names we call home: Auto-biography on racial identity*, New York: Routledge.

Freire, P. (1969) *Pedagogy of the oppressed: 30th anniversary edition*, trans. M. Bergman Ramos (2006), New York: Continuum.

Green, M. (2004) "Imagination, oppression, and culture: Creating authentic openings," paper presented at the Interrupting Oppression and Sustaining Justice Conference, New York.

Henry, M. (1999) "The player and the playing: An interpretive study of Richard Court-ney's texts on learning through drama," unpublished doctoral dissertation, New York University.

——(2000) "Drama's ways of learning," *Research in Drama Education: The Journal of Applied Theatre and Performance*, 5(1): 45–62.

hooks, b. (1990) *Yearning: Race, gender, and cultural politics*, Cambridge, MA: South End Press.

——(2003) *Teaching community: A pedagogy of hope*, New York: Routledge.

Hughes, J. and Wilson, K. (2004) "Playing a part: The impact of youth theatre on young people's personal and social development," *Research in Drama Education: The Jour-nal of Applied Theatre and Performance*, 9(1): 57–72.

Hunter, M. "What is design and why it matters." <http://www.thecreativeindustries.co.uk/uk-creative-overview/news-and-views/view-what-is-design-and-why-it-matters> (accessed March 5, 2013).

Jocson, K. M. (2008) "Situating the personal in digital media production," in M. L. Hill and L. Vasudevan (eds.), *Media, learning, and sites of possibility*, New York: Peter Lang.

Lambert, J. (2002) *Digital storytelling: Capturing lives, creating community*, Berkeley CA: Life on the Water.

——(2010) *Digital storytelling cookbook*, Digital Diner Press. <http://www.storycenter.org/storage/publications/cookbook.pdf> (accessed November 10, 2012).

Lerman, L. and Borstel, J. (2003) *Liz Lerman's critical response process: A method for getting useful feedback on anything you make, from dance to dessert*, Washington, DC: Dance Exchange.

Lundby, K. (2009) "The matrices of digital storytelling: Examples from Scandinavia," in J. Hartley and K. McWilliam (eds.), *Story circle: Digital storytelling around the world*, Malden, MA: Wiley-Blackwell.

Neelands, J. and Goode, T. (1990) *Structuring drama work: A handbook of available forms in theatre and drama*, Cambridge: Cambridge University Press.

Nicholson, H. (2009) "Re-locating memory: Performance, reminiscence and communities of diaspora," in T. Prentki and S. Preston (eds.), *The applied theatre reader*, New York: Routledge.

Perry, M. (2011) "Theatre and knowing: Considering the pedagogical spaces in devised theatre," *Youth Theatre Journal*, 25: 63–74.

Phelan, P. (1997) *Mourning sex: Performing public memories*, London: Routledge.

Resources for Learning (2012) "Gutenberg revisited: How art teaches the next form of literacy," PowerPoint presentation at the Center for Educator Development in Fine Arts Summit, Austin, TX.

Roberts, R. A. (2005) *Radical movements: Katherine Dunham and Ronald K. Brown teaching toward critical consciousness*, City University of New York Graduate Center, New York.

Rowe, A. C. (2008) *Power lines: On the subject of feminist alliances*, London: Duke University Press.

——(2009) "Moving relations: On the limits of belonging," *Liminalities: A Journal of Performance Studies*, 5(5). <http://liminalities.net/5-4/movingrelations.pdf> (accessed April 12, 2013).

Thompson, A. (1997) "For: Anti-racist education," *Curriculum Inquiry*, 27(1).

Thompson, J. (1999) *Drama workshops for anger management and offending behaviour*, London: Jessica Kingsley.

——(2003) *Applied theatre: Bewilderment and beyond*, New York: Peter Lang.

——(2009) *Performance affects: Applied theatre and the end of effect*, Basingstoke, UK: Palgrave Macmillan.

Watkins, J. and Russo, A. (2009) "Beyond individual expression: Working with cultural institutions," in J. Hartley and K. McWilliam (eds.), *Story circle: Digital storytelling around the world*, Malden, MA: Wiley-Blackwell, 267–278.

Weber, S. and Mitchell, C. (2008) "Imaging, keyboarding, and posting identities: young people and new media technologies," in D. Buckingham (ed.), *Youth, identity, and digital media*, Cambridge, MA: MIT Press.

Wissman, K. K. (2008) "'This is what I see': (Re)envisioning photography as social practice," in M. L. Hill and L. Vasudevan (eds.), *Media, learning, and sites of possibility*, New York: Peter Lang.

4 Inviting dialogue and deliberation with audiences

Something is happening here

The recreation room was packed with people from the community. A Native American "Coming Home" song played under the rolling credits and the audience applauded loudly as we turned the projector off. The youth participants—who were scattered around the space—made their way toward the front of the room for a short talkback. Several members of the audience stood up and congratulated the youth on their work, expressing an appreciation of the quality of the digital performance piece and the commitment required to follow through with such a long-term project. One Elder responded strongly to a specific moment in the movie: "It is a shame to not know our native language. I will come to the school and teach you, if you want to learn. Many of us believed you didn't have an interest in it." I remember thinking, "Something is happening here."

As I've written about in *Teaching Artist Journal* (Alrutz 2006) and *Stage of the Art* (Woodson *et al.* 2006), I spent over two years as a teaching artist with a program called Place: Vision, & Voice. During this time, I partnered with Stephani Etheridge Woodson and worked with Akimel O'otham and Pee Posh high school students on the Gila River Indian Community (an Indian reservation commonly referred to as GRIC and/or the Rez), located just outside of Phoenix, AZ. Rooted in conversations with GRIC's newly emerging Huhugam Heritage Center, our first residency with the students surrounded notions of heritage and identity; using theatre, creative writing, and digital media, young participants articulated stories and ideas about their own relationships to and understandings of heritage. In our first year on the Rez, the youths developed a 40-minute digital video that included a series of personal stories, photographs, interviews, poems, and artistic explorations around questions such as "What does heritage mean to you?" and "What does it mean to be Native American?" In grappling with notions of heritage, the young participants chose to represent a wide range of experiences from growing up on the Rez, including memories of their early years, relationships and struggles with Elders, and personal negotiations surrounding Native American traditions, language, and culture. The students' choice to celebrate, question, and sometimes challenge their relationships to traditional notions of heritage ultimately contributed to an aesthetically and emotionally dynamic video. However, the very personal and public nature of their artistic explorations also raised questions and tensions when shared with local audiences and authority figures in the community.

Following the initial showing in the high school's recreation room, the video—*The River People* (Akimel O'otham)—was accepted into an international film festival. The youth participants approached their Tribal Council for funding to attend the festival and present their work for a wider audience. In viewing *The River People* for this purpose, the Elders on the council, some of whom attended the initial showing, invited the youths and our creative team to a meeting. Several of the council members expressed concerns about the content of the video and others reprimanded the youths for how they represented the Rez and Native American culture in the piece. For many of the Elders, the youths' choice to represent drinking, drugging, and violence on the Rez (demonstrated in a few of the youths' poems and interviews), as well as an aesthetic decision to use a traditional "Coming Home" (or ending) song at the *beginning* of the video, proved irresponsible. Although some of the youths' choices in the video may have been brazen attempts to use performance (or public representation) to resist authority, many pieces of the video represented the youths' lived experiences from their perspective. Moreover, the placement of the "Coming Home" song pointed to the circular nature of heritage and culture as it passes to and from various generations. For the Elders, however, those choices foregrounded Native American youths disrespecting the Rez, their families, and their culture by publicly airing dirty laundry and ignorantly misusing a piece of cultural tradition. After sharing their views about the digital video, the council members deliberated behind closed doors about whether or not to financially support the group in attending a public viewing of *The River People* in another state. Waiting in the lobby with the youths, I remember thinking (again), "Something is happening here."

The tensions over language, ownership, and subsequent representation and reproduction of culture and knowledge beg many questions related to the public performance of personal stories. Who can and should share what stories? When working with young people, who has the authority to decide what they should represent in performance? How do youth-allies support young people to explore and question truths and experiences in their lives, while remaining respectful of cultural ideologies and systems of power/authority that exist to protect young people and/or cultural capital? And more to the focus of this chapter, how—as teaching artists—do we create spaces for meaningful dialogue and deliberation between youth participants and their audiences? How might we intentionally engage audiences around the questions raised in or by youths' performance work and continue working toward alliances?

We eventually rejoined the council members in their conference room. The general rhetoric returned to concerns around sharing negative representations of the Rez for an external audience. Several council members argued that given the general lack of Native American representation in theatre and film at large, *The*

River People could likely serve as an audience's first or only exposure to GRIC or narratives about Native American heritage and culture. Eventually, a grandparent of one of the youths, who was also a member of the council, stood up near the head of the table and agreed with the challenges expressed by his colleagues. He then followed up with questions about the responsibility of the Elders in this situation. He shared that *if* the youths inappropriately used a traditional tribal song in the video, then perhaps it signified a failure on the part of the Elders to communicate with young people about responsibilities around their heritage and traditions. He also argued that *if* the youths disrespected their tribe by discussing drinking, drugging, and violence on GRIC, then perhaps the Elders should engage young people in a more private sphere regarding these challenges. Speaking as an Elder, this grandparent articulated the importance of addressing places where different generations meet and where values and identities often diverge, points that seemed agreeable to the adults around the table. Although the Tribal Council eventually funded the youths' travel to the film festival and some important ideas emerged around the table, at that time, our performance ensemble did not actively participate in a dialogue about those places of divergence. Most of the conversation was held by the council members at the table—about the youths who sat largely silent in the room.

Listening to the Elders and working with the youth participants foregrounded the complexities at play in this situation and in larger efforts to build alliances across power lines. It made me reconsider my own role in this work, namely what it looks like to become both a youth-allied adult and a white-ally with an indigenous community.[1] As I experienced some of my own desires and values around youth wisdom and participation conflict with those of the Tribal Council, I became increasingly reflective about the various power lines at play in performing and distributing digital stories. What happens with a digital story once it is created? How and where are they performed, shared, or otherwise distributed? Who is impacted, and in what ways, by various representations and subsequent performances of those representations? How might the very practices that frame the creative development process also work to engage an audience with youths' stories, youths themselves, and these larger questions around culture, responsible representation, and allyship? Although something was happening in the room during both showings of *The River People*, how might participatory, applied theatre practices extend the dialogue, deliberation, and alliance-building in the room and beyond our intentional community of practice? In this case, we did not invite our audiences to participate in the kind of engagements that were central to our creative process. Instead, we practiced more traditional ways of sharing and viewing performance work—a practice that emphasized the audience's role as viewer/respondent/critic, rather than an interactive participant in a creative process or dialogue.

In Chapter 3, I addressed the role of dialogue and deliberation within the production or making of a digital story with an intentional community of practice. This chapter moves toward the presentation, performance, or screening of digital stories, attending to how we intentionally share mediated performance work with live, external audiences. To this end, I propose practical and theoretical frameworks for presenting digital stories in public and semi-public settings with the explicit desire to foster dialogue and deliberation between youth and their invited audience members. These frameworks come directly from my experiences with applied theatre praxis and young people, and draw on participatory practices from theatre and drama in education. While I have explored these practices in digital storytelling settings, many of the ideas I propose in this chapter will benefit from additional experimentation and study as part of digital storytelling engagements, events, and screenings. Many opportunities exist for integrating participatory media and theatre practices with young people, and I offer a small sample of ideas in this chapter.

Affective engagements

As put forward in earlier chapters, I approach digital storytelling as an applied theatre practice with fairly utopian goals for a more equitable society. I believe the arts play an important role in creating the possibility for equitable systems and spaces for democratic participation, while addressing the power systems at work within the performance process. However, in my practice at large and as I write this chapter now, I remain aware of the politics of participation and participatory arts practices. I share many scholars' discomfort with ambitious narratives around personal or social transformation in applied theatre spaces, as well as emancipatory narratives around interactivity and participation in and of itself. Helen Nicholson contends that while applied theatre is motivated by the "desire to make a difference to the lives of others" (2005: 16), challenges exist around describing drama's impact as transformative. She rightly reminds her readers to question how power functions in goals of transformation, specifically who and what gets transformed and by whom. In some ways, her critique offers freedom from the restraints that come with focusing only on the transformative potentials, or effects, of applied theatre, inviting facilitators to attend to affective engagements and how digital stories are shown, performed, experienced, and discussed in the room.

James Thompson (2009), in *Performance affects: Applied theatre and the end of effect*, theorizes about the field's current obsession with effects, impacts, and outcomes of applied theatre, i.e. measurable social outcomes such as decreases in teen pregnancy. Thompson posits that in placing more of an emphasis on the artistic encounter, which I argue is an effect in and of itself, we are able to imagine "the joy—the buzz—of the participatory arts as inseparable from the total impact of the event. The sensation is no longer the adjunct, the expendable adjective, but the dynamic texture of the work through which it finds its force" (2009: 131–132). In other words, participants and audiences, as well as the performance itself, might benefit from attention to the feelings or experience of an artistic encounter itself. Here, I imagine how framing audience participation in an applied performance event, as well as their aesthetic engagement with digital stories, may in fact begin to create conditions for the possibility of more permanent transformations or utopian visions for engaging with young people. And more immediately, this practice may also create possibilities for furthering relational engagements and practices, or meaningful interactions, between youth performance-makers and their audiences.

I often invoke two theories of change, namely *transportation* (Nicholson 2005; Schechner 2003) and *transgression* (hooks 1994) in my applied theatre praxis. These theories focus on individuals' experiences, actions, and movement, and they help me develop and frame, if not extend, affective engagements with and for digital storytelling audiences. Nicholson draws on Richard Schechner (2003) to suggest that applied theatre's possibilities for making a difference in the world lie in experiences of "transportation," or briefly moving into another world and experiencing something new, rather than in transformation. She argues that "transportation ... is less fixed—performers are 'taken somewhere,' actors are even temporarily transformed, but they are returned more or less to their starting places at the end of the drama or performance" (2005: 12). hooks points to critically engaged pedagogies as pathways through and against racism, sexism, and classism. In *Teaching to transgress*, hooks explains that she "celebrate[s] teaching that enables transgressions—a movement against and beyond boundaries. It is that movement which makes education the practice of freedom" (1994: 12). While in some ways pointing to desired, long-term *effects*, transportation and transgression also attend to affect. They each signify an experience, a feeling, and an encounter, rather than simply a measurable change or outcome. Moreover, they suggest movement on the part of the participant or the performer, or in the case of hooks, individuals involved in a learning experience.

With this in mind, I am interested in how a participatory, applied theatre performance or the framing of a performance or sharing itself offers opportunities for imagining one's self or situation anew (transportation) *and* crossing or pushing against oppressive borders that relate to one's thinking, experiences, or actions (transgression). As I've stated earlier in this text, goals of critical consciousness often underpin applied theatre and digital storytelling efforts, but with a particular emphasis on the participants in the process and on social change outcomes. In the sections that follow, I explore the possibility of what I call transgressive transportation, or critically engaged, aesthetic experiences that create conditions for imagining, exploring, and creating new places, images, ideas, and possibilities. This participatory practice sets the stage for aesthetic interactions between youth participants and audiences who presumably are invested in their stories and their lives.

Dramaturgy of audience participation: frameworks for dialogue and deliberation

As an applied theatre artist, I often blur the lines between drama-based practices designed for work *with* young participants and those I employ in professional theatre settings or performance engagements. For example, when devising performance work with young people, I use an embodied reflection tool called Spectrum of Difference (see Appendix C) to invite young participants to bring their perspective into the room, explore the meaning of a story, comment on a character, or debate a particular idea. The embodied act of standing and placing one's body on a continuum in response to information or debatable statements followed by a discussion on the various points of view represented in the group offers similar opportunities for audiences who view a presentational performance to bring their own experiences and perspectives into that performance event. Inviting audiences to share their perspectives, impressions, and questions *with* (and not simply *to*) young digital storytellers can shape the ways that audiences and young participants respond to and experience digital stories. To this end, I employ conventions from my applied theatre practice as frameworks for engaging live, digital storytelling audiences in dialogue with youth participants.

In his book *Audience Participation in Theatre: Aesthetics of the Invitation*, Gareth White focuses on procedural authorship, or the practice and process of inviting audiences to participate in a theatre performance. In doing so, he "treats audience participation as art" (2013: 197) and offers possibilities for extending affective engagements beyond the presentational aspects of a digital storytelling event. Drawing on such possibilities, I emphasize the aesthetic experience of the youth participants and their audiences throughout the performance event. This participation includes traditional spectatorship, such as watching a play from the audience seating area, and invites new stories, perspectives, and experiences from the audience to shape the larger aesthetic encounter with the performance event and the other people in the room. While digital storytelling as a performance form does not necessarily warrant interactivity or participation that explicitly impacts the action of the digital stories, it does invite possibilities for dialogue and deliberation with and among audience members. The audience's participation is integral to how everyone experiences the performance event as a whole.

Within digital storytelling as an applied theatre practice, the challenge becomes how to integrate aesthetically engaging, face-to-face encounters[2] or participation *with* the screening of digital stories. In proposing such encounters within a digital storytelling performance, I find Anthony R. Jackson's (1997) writing on participatory frames within theatre-in-education (TIE) particularly useful. Jackson employs Erving Goffman's (1974) theories on frame analysis and the social construction of experiences to name and analyze various stages and structures of audience involvement with a performed story, play, and/or workshop aimed at student audiences in a school setting. Applying Goffman's frame analysis to TIE, Jackson posits that

> [a frame] is often used to describe a key feature of any performed work of art—that which makes it art rather than the flux of everyday life. The theatrical frame could be said to consist of the boundary line, visible or invisible, that theatre artists deliberately draw around the piece of

experience that they wish to highlight or to examine. That boundary line enables the artist to craft the action within it in ways that intensify and give particular significance to aspects of human experience.

(1997: 55)

In other words, we can use theatrical and aesthetic frames to foreground a particular moment or experience as significant in some way. Facilitators and youth participants, then, can attend to, and possibly structure, an audience's participation in performance work as aesthetically or otherwise meaningful. Like White, Jackson's writing on TIE emphasizes a complete aesthetic frame-work, one that "encompass[es] the totality of the performance event: the artis-try and the reception by and the engagement of the audience—which draws on that sensibility and allows the actors and audience to meet on metaphoric ground" (1997: 52). While I am thinking less about professional actors and student or school-based audiences, and instead about youth performance-makers and their invited audiences, Jackson's attention to the whole theatrical event as an aesthetic framework points to the variety of ways that an audience might participate in, at, and during a performance, ways that move beyond simply the presentational elements of performance. Participatory and interactive frames throughout a performance event can become as significant to the audi-ence's experiences as the presentational elements of a performance.

Jackson discusses a variety of frames that I categorize into two distinct types or sets for considering audience participation. The first set of frames, which I delineate as sequence-based frames, refers to the somewhat linear timeline of engaging audience members in a performance event, including the moment they are introduced to a performance (the pre-theatre frame) through the moment they leave the performance event (the closing frame). The second set of frames, which I refer to as experiential or action frames, explain the nature of the audience's participation at various points throughout the timeline, such as whether they listen to a verbal curtain speech (narrative frame), watch a per-formance (presentational frame), directly interact with the performance-makers (involvement frame), etc. Here, I provide two tables outlining Jackson's TIE frames within these sequence-based and experiential or action categories (see Table 4.1 and Table 4.2).

A traditional theatre event, such as attending a play in a professional theatre setting, may focus primarily on a presentational frame (experience-based) within the inner frame (sequence-based). Jackson's analysis of TIE demon-strates broader ways of thinking about the relationships between performers, a performance, and the audience. Through charts of his own and a careful ana-lysis of a TIE performance, he explains how within the inner frame of a TIE performance, the audience may in fact participate in a variety of actions that move beyond viewing the presentation itself, such as investigating a question or theme posed by the presentation (Jackson 1997: 57–59).

I take Jackson's analytical framework for TIE a step further and argue that his variety of functional frameworks, or experiential and action frames, can be

Table 4.1 Sequence-based Frames in TIE

Type of Frame	Description
Pre-theatre Frame	"The explicit preparation for the drama that may be done by the teacher or the actor out of role … It may happen in or outside the stage space and in the moments (or even several days) before the action begins" (Jackson 1997: 57).
Outer Theatrical Frame	"The establishment of the theatrical space and conventions that will apply, usually done by the first actor to appear or through use of the lights, music, etc. Clear signaling of the start of the performance" (Jackson 1997: 57).
Inner Frames	The performers activate the "theatre frame proper: the performance begins; the students are positioned as the audience. Their positioning, however, is quickly given a functional dimension" (Jackson 1997: 56).
Closing Frame	"The formal end of the overall theatre event and clearly signaled as such, e.g. by speech, music, silence, tableau, lights. Usually a return to [the outer frame]" (Jackson 1997: 57). The audience returns to everyday contexts.

Table 4.2 Experiential or Action Frames in TIE

Type of Frame	Description
Investigative Frame	"Events may occur in 'real time' with pupils in midst, or as evidence to be analysed & discussed (e.g. flash-backs or still images). A facilitator will usually initiate & link the events and chair debate" (Jackson 1997: 58).
Involvement Frame	"Interplay between characters and between characters and students as events unfold. Usually naturalistic & in 'real time'. Characters + students occupy same acting area" (Jackson 1997: 58).
Narrative Frame	"Events, background & issues of the drama are introduced & recounted by Narrator or Facilitator—especially to provide a 'holding' frame for the drama & establish/reinforce conventions. Sometimes in the form of direct address by characters within the frame" (Jackson 1997: 58).
Presentational Frame	"Events enacted by actors in role-characters as in conventional play. Often naturalistic but may be stylized (expressionistic, 'epic,' etc). Stage area clearly defined but may be end-on, in-round, etc." (Jackson 1997: 58).

applied within each of the sequence-based frames, and not simply within the inner frame—a significant focus of Jackson's analysis. Imagining how experiential frames apply to every stage of the performance event can expand how we engage audiences and young performance-makers in dialogue and deliberation. Below, I build on and revise Jackson's sequence-based frames specifically to attend to a participatory digital storytelling event. I then demonstrate how various applied theatre activities serve as practical ways to structure audience engagement at various points throughout the performance event.

In Table 4.3 and Table 4.4, I rename some of Jackson's frames to move beyond references to TIE and student audiences, and to include participatory engagements with digital stories and performance at large. I add an additional sequence frame, the outer performance frame II, to acknowledge that within many participatory performance events the audience moves through an outer frame to the inner frame and then back through an outer frame again before the closing frame. I also add an additional action frame, the responsive frame, to recognize that audiences might contribute artifacts or ideas within the performance event that may not be read, consumed, or experienced by the youth participants until the event ends. Lastly, I include revised descriptions of several of Jackson's frames in order to broadly focus on adult and family audiences and contexts rather than simply student audiences and/or curricular contexts of TIE.

With these two sets of frames, I am interested in practical engagements and activities that prompt audiences to intentionally consider their encounter with a performance and to interact with youth performance-makers in meaningful ways. Just as I aim to create room for young participants to bring their lived experiences into the devising process, I want to extend a similar invitation to audiences who attend a digital storytelling screening or performance. This practice, or invitation, can be initiated on an individual basis and/or as a more collective activity. Either way, in crafting a series of invitations for the audience to engage within a digital story performance, I focus on what Winston and Strand call the "playful aesthetic" of applied theatre (2013: 63). They suggest that within their own work the aesthetic of applied theatre supports the airing and discussing of ideas in a "civil yet provocative manner" (Winston and Strand 2013: 63).

Through a variety of applied theatre activities, I aim to provoke feelings and thought, as well as make space for audiences and youth participants to interact with one another in new or embodied ways. With an eye toward theatricality and interactivity, I often frame audience engagement through a series of questions, embodied and performative activities, or some kind of gesture of sharing. I also consider how various invitations, experiences, and activities might fit within each sequence-based frame. While I discuss specific applied theatre activities for each sequence-based frame, many of these activities can be applied at various points in a performance sequence. Where and how each activity is located in the performance event may change the intention or outcome, as well as the ways that audiences and youth participants engage with each other and in the event as a whole.

Table 4.3 Sequence-based Frames in Digital Storytelling as an Applied Theatre Practice

Type of Sequence-based Frame	Description
Pre-performance Frame	The moment of initial invitation or how the performance event, including the form and content, is communicated to the audience.
Outer Performance Frame I	The period of time when the performance space and its conventions are established, and the audience is intentionally invited to consider their relationship to the form and content of the performance or the performance-makers.
Inner Performance Frame	The period of time when the audience experiences the digital stories or live performance pieces developed by the youth performance-makers.
Outer Performance Frame II	The period of time following the sharing of digital stories or live performance pieces that may include additional invitations to relate their own lives and experiences to and with those of the youth performance-makers.
Closing Frame	The moment that the performance event comes to a closing point.

Table 4.4 Experiential or Action Frames in Digital Storytelling as an Applied Theatre Practice

Type of Experience	Description	Examples
Investigative Frames	Audiences explore a theme or topic, building connections between their own lives and the form/content of the performance.	Gallery Walk Photo on the Wall It Made Me Think Q & A with facilitator
Involvement Frames	Audiences directly engage with youth performance-makers in dialogue and/or a creative and embodied activity/process. Audiences may contribute, share, or perform aesthetic material, such as digital photographs, creative writing, stories, or soundscapes, to the performance event.	Digital Postcard Hot Seating Graffiti Alphabet Six-Word Stories Social Media Posts Think/Pair/Share Vote From Your Seat
Narrative Frames	Audiences are introduced to background information about the performance. Often includes direct address from a facilitator or performance-maker.	Written Invitation Narrative Flyer Press Release Direct Address From Facilitator
Presentational Frames	Audiences are often separated from a clearly delineated stage or screening area and positioned to view digital stories or a live performance.	Audio Collage Digital Stories Installation Performance Trailers Live Scenes or Monologues
Responsive Frames	Audiences leave an artifact or trace of their thoughts or ideas in response to the performance event. Youth performers do not usually engage with this material until the performance event has ended.	Poster Dialogue Response Ribbons Social Media Posts

To put these frames and activities in context, I explore possibilities for structuring audience engagement within different programs, including the Performing Justice Project (PJP),[3] an applied performance program that I co-direct with Lynn Hoare in Austin, TX. In a recent project with young women in incarceration, the youth participants devised a live and mediated performance piece based on their own life experiences related to gender and racial justice. Borrowing the structure of Michele Norris's Race Card Project (Norris "About"), the youths wrote six-word stories about their relationship to race and/or gender. Several of these six-word stories became longer monologues, scenes, audio stories, and movement sequences in the performance itself. And, as the audience entered the space to view the performance (outer performance frame I), the ushers invited them to read 3' x 5' posters on the walls that displayed the youths' six-word stories—written, drawn, and otherwise decorated or embellished with markers. Through an investigative frame called Gallery Walk, this visual display of the youths' stories invited the audience to walk around the room and explore the youths' stories at their own pace and actively or intentionally relate their own lives to the themes, feelings, and questions put forward by the performance-makers.

In this PJP example, our pre-performance frame consisted of a paper invitation/flyer that employed a narrative frame to introduce our target audience to basic information, such as the title and time of the performance, as well as some of the rules regulating outsiders' visitation to the juvenile justice facility. Looking back, this pre-performance frame might have aligned further with our performance in some interesting ways. Digital storytelling and applied theatre offer a variety of performative and experiential structures for reimagining typical approaches to the pre-performance frame. A presentational frame—for example, such as an emailed audio collage of youth stories or a video trailer with sample material from the performance, or an investigative frame such as a digital postcard with a written note and a provocative question—might also encourage the audience to reflect on their own gender or racial identity prior to attending the performance.

As audiences move from the pre-performance frame to the outer performance frame I, many possibilities exist for inviting the audience to participate in or engage with the event. As mentioned above, we used an activity called Gallery Walk, or an intentional engagement with displayed images, words, or objects, to encourage the audience to explore a question or topic from the performance (investigative frame). In future iterations of this outer performance frame, I might involve the audience on different levels. For example, following the Gallery Walk, as people take their seats to view the performance, I might lead a round of Vote from Your Seat (see Appendix C) to move audiences through an involvement frame prior to the presentation. In this exercise, I—or the youth performers—read a series of statements, one at a time, out loud to the audience. We construct the statements in the first person and we invite the audience to embody their response to each statement. For example, if the audience agrees with the statement read aloud, they stand up at their seat. If they disagree with the statement, they remain seated. The statements are designed to encourage the audience to reflect on themes presented throughout the performance event and also help the performance-makers take stock of prior knowledge or beliefs held by participants in the room. In the instance of this particular PJP event, we could have invited the audience to embody responses to the following types of statements:

1. The stories on the wall made me think about my own life.
2. My gender impacts my life on a daily basis.
3. My racial and ethnic identity is rarely on my mind.
4. The justice system is color-blind.
5. Stories can make change in the world.

These kinds of statements have no right or wrong answer and offer debatable positions for the audience to consider. Sometimes I invite less polarized responses, such as "undecided" or "both yes and no," which audiences embody by standing with bent knees or with one knee on their chair, rather than standing fully upright or sitting fully in their chair. Other times, I limit the activity to yes and no responses as a playful challenge to unpack difficult questions or underscore the key area of debate. Either way, Vote from Your Seat can be adjusted to include less movement, such as raising or lowering one's arms to indicate agreement/disagreement, or more movement, such as placing one's body on different sides of the room to embody a particular response.

After the audience members respond to a statement by sitting down, standing up, or embodying a position somewhere in between, I invite a few individuals from each response group (yes, no, maybe) to explain their position or thinking behind their embodied vote. At this time, the audience and the youth participants in the room begin to entertain a variety of perspectives and experiences, and, ideally, we all consider how our own responses relate to those of others in the room. Following each round of Vote from Your Seat, including the participants' brief explanations and possible group discussion, the participants vote again, responding to the same statement after various positions have been explained or justified by people in the room. Participants in the activity may shift their physical position—their vote—if their own relationship to the statement at hand has changed. This process exemplifies what Fuchs and De Jaegher describe as "participatory sense-making—the process of generating and transforming meaning in the interplay of interacting individuals and the interaction process itself" (2009: 466).

In addition to participating in Vote from Your Seat, the audience might also generate a creative product as another way to relate their own lives to the content of the performance. For example, in the PJP performance mentioned above, we could have invited audiences to create and share their own six-word stories, cell phone photos, and/or social media content, following their Gallery Walk through the youths' posters. In structuring an involvement frame, each audience member might receive a blank notecard along with a verbal, printed, or projected invitation (narrative frame) to write their own six-word story about their relationship to gender, race, or justice. These short, often poetic stories might then be exchanged or shared with someone sitting next to them, collected and shared out as part of the performance, and/or anonymously taped to the wall beside the youths' storied posters.

Whether the stories are shared publicly or not, the act of considering one's relationship to race and gender through the creation of a six-word story mirrors the youths' creative process and invites the audience to reflect on the content of the performance event as a whole. Placed within the outer performance frame I, these activities also set the stage for the audience to engage with ideas that underpin the youths' work and ultimately inform the form and content of their digital stories.

In an effort to further interactivity, I sometimes invite audiences to produce or explore photographs and visual images prior to or immediately following a screening of digital stories (outer performance frames I and II). I facilitate an activity called Photo on the Wall (see Appendix C) to invite imaginative thinking and set up anticipation around, and personal connections to, the form and content of the performance event. In this activity, images or photographs of people (representing a wide variety of identity markers, such as age, ethnicity, and gender) hang on the walls around the space. These images might come from the digital stories themselves or simply be related to the stories through aesthetic or form.

Through the framework of a Gallery Walk, the audience moves around the periphery of the room viewing the images at their own pace and in their own desired order. After about five or ten minutes, the youth participants or the facilitator invite the audience to choose one image they felt drawn to in some way during their Gallery Walk. Each audience member then removes their chosen image from the wall and takes it with them as they take a seat for the performance. In this moment, each audience member presumably has an image in their hands that sparked their interest. As part of the interpretive frame, the audience members each engaged with all or some of the images scattered throughout the room, and they participated in an affective experience as they recognized or built a personal connection to a visual image. Photo on the Wall offers audiences a concrete object to reflect on prior to the presentational elements of the performance and also sets up common experience among the audience members.

To move Photo on the Wall into an involvement frame prior to the screening of digital stories, I employ reflection questions and an activity called Think, Pair, Share (see Appendix C) to encourage engagement with the form of the performance (images/video) they are about to see and with the youth participants in the room. The audience first considers the questions on an individual basis (think), and then reflects on them in pairs or with a small group of people seated near them (pair). Finally, each pair shares with the larger group one image and one big idea that came up in their dialogue (share). Here is a list of sample reflection questions I use with Photo on the Wall.

1. *Describe*: Why did you choose this image? What were you drawn to?
2. *Describe*: What is going on in the image you've chosen? What do you see?

3. *Analyze*: What do you imagine the person in this photograph is thinking about or experiencing at the time the image was captured?

4. *Analyze*: What do you imagine this person dreams about for the future?

5. *Analyze*: If one person or thing was holding this individual back from realizing that dream or future, who/what might that be?

6. *Analyze*: If one person or thing was supporting this individual in reaching that dream or future, who/what might that be?

7. *Reflect*: Based on what you can see or imagine, what might you have in common with the individual in this photograph? How might your lives or experiences be different?

8. *Relate*: The title of our performance is "What is Justice?" How might you title the image or photograph that you have in your hands? How might justice apply to the individual in your image?

When youth participants engage in Photo on the Wall simultaneously with the audience, opportunities arise for dialogue and deliberation between the two groups. Reflecting silently and then with others about an image can transform that image into a storied or meaningful object, and ultimately frame an affective engagement for the audience. This outer performance frame focuses attention first on an aesthetic object, then on self, and finally on the ideas put forward by others. By reflecting on and relating to the photograph with another person, an opportunity arises to share and gain information about one another, and to discuss various points of view and/or deliberate about the stories or narratives present in a visual representation. Moreover, the audience begins to experience how applied performance work and digital storytelling can develop from visual inspiration, storied images and objects, and group dialogue. Importantly, this approach to Photo on the Wall invites people to focus their attention, feelings, and ideas on an object (the photograph), rather than talk about themselves off the cuff. In this way, the photograph becomes the nexus of the affective engagement.

Social media outlets can also offer additional aesthetic opportunities for outer performance frames of engagement at a digital storytelling event.[4] As audience members enter the performance space or take their seats to watch digital stories created by young people, I often pose a question or a prompt related to the performance, such as "I believe justice is _____" or "What does justice look like?" In addition to asking the questions, I might invite the audience to respond with a text message, tweet, or Facebook post. Moving beyond language-based responses, I sometimes encourage a visual response, such as capturing and posting a photo to Instagram or Facebook, a short video to Vine, or a check-in (mapped location) on Facebook. These types of language-, idea-, and image-based responses can be posted to an audience member's own social media accounts and shared with already familiar contacts, friends, and readers. However, I might also invite the audience to join and respond to an online account managed by the youth performance ensemble. In this case, for example, a Twitter or Instagram feed started by the performance group may be projected onto a screen in the performance space itself, showing a variety of real-time photos or responses posted by people in the room. The immediate posting of responses from the audience can promote a virtual conversation with the audience's friends or family outside of the performance space or contribute directly to the performance event itself through an active stream of texts, tweets, status updates, or other image-based posts (involvement frame). Each of these activities support the interactivity of an involvement frame, which can be employed in the outer performance frames, as described here, or in other sequence-based frames throughout the performance.

Activities offered in the pre-performance and outer performance frame I, such as the few ideas discussed here, offer the audience a way into participatory performance settings. While none of these activities requires participation from everyone in the audience, they certainly accommodate the possibility for large audiences to begin experiencing and engaging with the form and content of digital stories and applied theatre, and thus understanding the context for youths' work. Moreover, they invite youth participants and their audiences to reimagine what it looks like to attend a performance event or a digital story-telling screening. Audience engagement can take many forms within each part of the sequence. Finally, these types of participatory frameworks can set the stage for viewing digital stories and experiencing an affective, and, thus, a potentially transporting and transgressing, relationship with the work and the youth creators.

While a variety of applied theatre frameworks may be employed during the inner performance frame, they can feel extraneous when woven throughout or within the actual screening of a digital story or a set of stories. However, if the form and content of a digital story or a series of digital stories allows for interactive participation, it often functions to inspire the audience to imagine the ending of a story or to identify some of the individual or systemic contexts shaping the action of the story. For example, digital stories might be used in educational or training settings that engage young people or people working with young people to imagine solutions or alternative paradigms for solving problems, such as bullying, peer pressure, or dealing with trauma. Schools might invite young people to create digital stories about a difficult decision or moral dilemma they faced at school. On screen, through a presentational frame, the student might recount his or her personal story, specifically setting up the scenario that led to a problem or a moment of critical decision-making.

After the problem or moment of decision is revealed, the facilitator sets up an investigative frame, pausing the digital story and inviting the viewers to discuss what they think will happen next in the presented scenario or moment of decision-making. Within this dialogue, the viewers investigate the story-teller's situation further and hypothesize about possibilities for handling the particular situation in light of the given circumstances and their own set of values and experiences. The audience describes the story or situation, analyzes the key details shaping the decision to be made at the height of the story's action, and brainstorms possibilities for moving forward or solving the problem at hand. Following these deliberations, the audience views the remainder of the digital story and the actual conclusion is revealed. While the audience does not in fact change or impact the narrative of the digital story itself (often a marker of audience participation in theatre), the story becomes an impetus for imagining new, possible endings or solutions to a problem, sharing lessons learned, and revealing complexities around actual crises and problems that arise in truly complex moments of decision-making. Here, the interactive participation within the inner performance frame is meant to impact positively the future decision-making of students.

Within the inner performance frame of a digital storytelling event, the audience participates in a presentational frame when watching the digital story, a narrative frame when the facilitator of the event explains the structure of the participation or verbally sets the stage for participation—such as the ideas that the audience will view a part of the digital story and then discuss possible solutions to the problem presented in the story. Followed by an investigative frame, the audience explores their own relationship to the critical questions presented by the digital story itself. In addition to these three types of inner frames, an involvement frame becomes possible when the digital storytellers themselves are in the room or present for direct involvement with the audience. For example, the storyteller might participate in a hot-seating activity, or a focused interview in which the audience asks questions of the live storyteller and obtains additional details about the story or the teller. Moreover, the audience might participate by sharing their ideas or questions, via social media, a written notecard, or a dialogue with the youth storytellers themselves. However the participation is structured within the inner performance frame, it involves direct interaction with the presentation of the digital story or stories, if not direct engagement with the storyteller(s).

Following the inner performance frame, the audience transitions into the outer performance frame II, during which a variety of action frames can be employed for the first time or once again after viewing the digital stories. By the time the audience moves into the outer performance frame II, the youths' digital stories have been presented and opportunities arise to dialogue and deliberate about what the youths created and how multiple digital stories, when curated for a performance event and shown together, offer insight into the youths' point of view, as well as questions or ideas about a theme, a community, or society at large. The outer performance frame II often includes traditional talkbacks with the audience, such as the one that took place following the Place: Vision & Voice screening described at the opening of this chapter. Here, I imagine how a couple of applied theatre frameworks might deepen dialogue and deliberation between audience members and youth performance-makers following a digital storytelling screening.

Although most of the audience members for youth digital storytelling screenings are often familiar with at least one youth participant in the process, the audience may not be familiar with one another or interested in public participation. So, facilitating meaningful interactions in outer performance frame II requires careful scaffolding of risk and participation. Years ago in a workshop with theatre-maker Michael Rohd, I learned to quickly reflect on a day's work by responding to the phrase "It made me think." He invited participants to stand in a circle, reflect on the creative time shared together, and say a word or phrase followed by "It made me think." This reflection tool uses a poetic framework to name several key moments and ideas from the day, and also to affirm that the variety of experiences and perspectives that come into the workshop impact, or make an impression on, the group. The framework of It Made Me Think also allows for a spectrum of direct and indirect responses from participants, mitigating some of the risk that comes with sharing personal reflections with a (perhaps) new group of people. When applied within the outer performance frame II of a digital storytelling performance, this technique serves a similar purpose, but with the added intention of including the audience. It Made Me Think can invite the audience and the youth participants to reflect on what they saw and experienced during the presentational screening or in earlier action frames. Participants and audience members distill that experience or moment into a word or phrase, and then share it with the group at large through the ritualized framework of the repeated phrase, "It made me think." Following a few digital storytelling screenings, I've employed this framework and heard reflections such as, "Perspective, it made me think," "Parental support, it made me think," "Our future, it made me think," "Consequences, it made think," "Representation of women, it made me think," and "Facing fear, it made me think." These reflections sometimes reference one particular digital story, but several comments at each screening tend to pick up on ideas or themes that run through several digital stories or on questions raised by the collection of digital stories as a whole. Depending on the size and comfort of the audience, I sometimes ask for volunteers to share their reflection with the group, rather than asking the entire group to share, one at a time.

Following a lower-risk investigative frame such as It Made Me Think, audiences might collaborate with youth participants in small groups to respond to a question or theme generated from the screened digital stories. If the presentational frame, for example, included several digital stories that touched on themes related to gender, I might invite the audience to consider this theme through a written poster-dialogue, a captured photograph, a frozen image or a tableau with their bodies, or an activity called Graffiti Alphabet. I facilitate a version of Graffiti Alphabet (see Appendix C) in which small groups gather at stations around the room. Each station includes markers or crayons, and six to ten pieces of blank paper scattered out over a table, in a concentrated area on the floor, or taped across a wall. Gathering at their own station, each small group randomly writes the letters of the alphabet onto the papers, as though the alphabet letters were tossed onto the surface and scattered across the surface of the pages. The letters can be written in different sizes, as small as a nickel or as large as a half-dollar, and in different fonts. Once the letters of the alphabet are written out, the group brainstorms words, phrases, ideas, themes, images, and questions that came up in the digital stories screened during the inner performance frame. The youth participants collaborate with audience members to write and/or draw their ideas across the pages, documenting one word, phrase, or image that begins with each letter of the alphabet. For example, in reflecting on stories about gender, the group might write "androgynous" next to the letter "A" on the page or draw a picture of a "bra" or a "female dog" next to or incorporating the letter "B." I encourage participants to employ visual clues, such as big and small print, thin and thick lines, and different colors, to express a point of view or to emphasize important ideas in their Graffiti Alphabet. Drawing on the history of graffiti art, I also encourage participants to consider how to visually represent underlying political or social messages in their graffiti work.

As each group moves through Graffiti Alphabet, the participants discuss what they recall from the digital stories and negotiate what they document and what ideas are emphasized across the pages. The participants systematically recall specific details from the digital stories and deliberate about their representation. Moreover, this activity invites youth participants and audience members to take on different roles. Some people draw, others write, and some verbally contribute through recall and response. Everyone has viewed the digital stories and begins the activity with a common experience to draw on. As they produce a Graffiti Alphabet, individuals begin to articulate their personal connections to and experiences with the digital stories.

After the pages are filled with the groups' ideas, I invite participants to arrange the various pieces of paper into an art installation. Each group considers how they want their art-filled pages to be read or experienced by others, as well as how the visual form, or the relationship of the pages to the space and to each other, might communicate an overarching idea about gender. Finally, in this involvement frame, each group titles their graffiti installation with a word or phrase and places a titled placard next to the installation.

At this point, each of the groups rotates throughout the room, spending two to three minutes at each installation, reading the words and images documented by other groups and reflecting on how each installation communicates new or familiar ideas about the digital stories presented. While at each installation, the viewing group members work together to choose one word, phrase, or image from the given installation that resonates with every member of their group. After the word, phrase, or image is chosen and shared out among the entire audience, the groups rotate to the next installation, repeating the previous exercise at each installation, or at as many installations as time permits, in a sense, naming and renaming their experiences with the youths' digital stories.

Moving through several installations and publicly responding with one word or phrase that resonates with an entire group requires dialogue and deliberation among the people at each installation. As part of this involvement frame, individuals contribute their own ideas and feelings about what has been presented and how it has been visually represented. They listen to the ideas and feelings of others in the group and then deliberate about how to collectively respond to the representations put forward by others at the event. In addition, this type of involvement frame invites the audience to bring their own life experiences to the performance event, rather than simply respond as critics to the youths' digital stories. In this way, the outer performance frame II becomes a space for involving the audience in conversation with the youth participants and creates opportunities to structure dialogue and deliberation with the audience as part of an affective experience. Moreover, the installations and each group's response to them become part of the larger performance event, which includes the screening of digital stories, as well as these generative and reflective creative practices.

I also facilitate an embodied activity called People to People (see Appendix C) to invite audiences and youth participants to interact with each other and explore ideas raised in the youths' digital stories. As the facilitator, I begin this involvement frame by inviting the audience and youth participants to find a partner in the room and to stand or sit back to back with that person. Once partners are established, I explain that People to People is a call-and-response activity; as I call out directions, I invite the group to respond physically or verbally, depending on the nature of the prompt. The main prompt, "People to People," signals for everyone to move silently and quickly to a new place in the room, find a new partner, and position themselves back to back with their new pair. I often call "People to People" several times in a row to mix up the group before moving on to additional prompts. I then add in physical prompts by calling out names of two body parts, such as "palms to palms" or "hands to shoulders." These prompts invite each pair to complete a task or collectively solve a problem, namely touching their palms together, or placing their hands on their partner's shoulders, etc., without talking. As the prompts get increasingly silly or difficult to accomplish, such as "toes to elbow" or "ear to knee," the pairs silently negotiate and problem-solve how they will respond to the call, while taking care of their own bodies and their partner in the process.[5] After the pairs respond to several different physical prompts, I call "People to People" again before announcing several new physical prompts.

After multiple rounds of partnering and varying levels of physical challenges, I call out a short discussion question or a verbal prompt for each pair to discuss for one minute. I follow each discussion question with "People to People," prompting individuals to find new partners and collaborate with multiple people throughout the activity. Discussion prompts within People to People might include the following types of questions:

1. Describe one moment or image that stood out to you from the digital stories.
2. What is one question that the digital stories raised for you?
3. Explain one idea from the digital stories that you can relate to and why.
4. Who else do you think should see these stories?
5. How do these stories relate to [insert theme, topic, or title here]?

Eventually, I systematically alternate calls of People to People, physical prompts, and verbal prompts. Playing with pacing and interspersing physical challenges, such as "elbow to big toe" or "pinky finger to earlobe," with reflection questions helps maintain audience engagement, as well as the playful aesthetic of applied theatre. To close this involvement frame, I often invite pairs to move into groups of four to six and create a tableau, or a frozen image based on a word or phrase from the title of the event or the collection of digital stories. People to People requires physical, verbal, and aesthetic participation of the audience, and this particular sequence intentionally scaffolds involvement from non-verbal to verbal participation, while slowly building dialogue between members of the audience and the youth participants. These types of movement, physicality, and interactions can be tailored to the youth participants and audiences of a given performance or screening event.

The closing frame, or the final button on the performance event, might be signaled by a change in lighting, music, or another sensory experience framed by the performance-makers. However, some action frames offer possibilities for participation that moves beyond presentational frames. In my own applied performance events, the closing frame often includes a responsive frame, or an activity that invites the audience to leave a thought or question in the space as they exit. I might include a written evaluation form for the audience to fill out or offer an aesthetic framework for commenting on the event as a whole or leaving the participants with a question to consider. For a performance such as the PJP event described here, I might facilitate It Made Me Think or position markers and posters by the exit with provocative questions or statements, such as "Today, I will enact justice by …" Through a final narrative frame, I would invite the audience to respond to the statements or questions by writing a word or phrase or drawing an image on the poster as they leave the performance. Some of my colleagues hang response ribbons from the ceiling outside the doors of a performance event, inviting audiences to write a general comment on a notecard and pin it to a hanging ribbon. More recently, I've seen facilitators invite audiences to post an architectural photo expressing a feeling on Facebook, Twitter, or Instagram at the closing of the performance. In an applied performance project called mappingDESIRE, a group of university-based performance-makers invited audiences to record an audio story that was later posted to an online map of the university campus. As part of a digital story-telling screening, these types of responses leave youth participants, and often their audiences, with a variety of new reflections and stories, many of which are sparked by the youths' digital stories, as well as contribute to an online dialogue following the event. In each case, the form and content of the closing frame often shapes final impressions and affective experiences for both the audience and the youth participants.[6]

Extending alliances with invited audiences

Unlike public audiences for traditional theatre performances or film, audiences for digital stories created by young people are often interested and invested in the lives of the youth participants on a personal or political level. Moreover, audience members usually attend digital storytelling screenings with the understanding that the youth performance-makers are not professional performers or media-makers. The audience tends to include family members, friends, teachers, public officials, or public groups with a particular connection to the youth ensemble, a specific youth participant, youth development in general, and/or the form or topic of the performance itself. In most cases, the youth have existing, if not ongoing, relations with someone in the audience. In facilitating participatory frames with such audiences, then, I aim to build on these relationships to foster dialogue and deliberation within the performance event. Admittedly, I hope these critical, embodied, and engaged dialogues create possibilities for ongoing reflexivity for the participants and audiences, as well as intergenerational alliances beyond the often short-term nature of digital storytelling performances and events.

Coming back to hooks and Nicholson, how do various action frames, such as those described above, create possibilities for transgressive transportation within a performance event? The devising of digital stories as outlined in Chapter 3 invites youth performance-makers to transgress or press against given ideas and representations as they imagine, create, experience, and understand themselves and their social/political circumstances in new ways. The critically engaged creative process offers opportunities for young people to disrupt fixed ideas and identities, as well as experiences, through their use of narrative, image, and performance. Fostering similar moments of transgressive transportation with an audience in a period of two or three hours presents a unique set of challenges. How, for example, might the presentation and brief exploration of youth's digital stories invite audiences to (re)consider the relationships between identity and power, or imagine and enact alliances with young people? How can a focus on affective engagements move into critical dialogue and action, even if that action is imagined, represented, or felt within moments of transportation?

Audiences often expect to enter a performance space and simply view the performance. Participatory activities such as Vote from Your Seat, People to People, or Gallery Walk can work to disrupt this normative status of the audience, as well as everyday interactions between youth participants and the audience. Traditional boundaries between the audience, the performance, and the performers do not explicitly invite or require audience members to consider their own identities, or to actively participate in dialogue about how their own experiences relate to those presented in the work of art. As seen in the examples throughout this chapter, action frames can build on existing relationships and expectations in the room, and also interrupt them by prompting a variety of critical and embodied interactions between young people and their audiences.

Applied theatre frameworks can set up spaces for the audience to share stories, discuss personal identities, and explore themes and perspectives put forward by the youth participants. They also can invite the audience into relational practices and create the conditions for critically engaged reflections on individual and systemic narratives. In addition, the participatory frames situate youth participants as experts—on the stories performed, their own lives, and explorations of identity and systems of power. Through the act of sharing and listening to each other's stories, the histories and experiences of people attending the performance become a set of contexts for seeing and understanding multiple and intersecting identities, if not systems of power at play across a community or society. "To hear each other (the sound of different voices), to listen to one another," bell hooks writes, "is an exercise in recognition" (1994: 41). This recognition—of both self and others—is necessary for creating the possibility of alliances among audiences, youth participants, and facilitators.

In reaching to build such alliances, I rely on the feminist concept of intersectionality, a theoretical framework for seeing how gender, ethnicity, class, sexuality, and other identity factors, with a particular focus on historically marginalized identities, shape our experiences of privilege and oppression. Rowe draws on Dorinne Kondo's (2000) work to argue that we "must attend to the movements of solidarity, empowerment, and accountability across multiple power lines" (2009: 4). Rowe's work suggests that building alliances between young people and their audiences requires attention to how power functions across and through power-laden identities, including mine, yours, theirs, and ours. As in the devising process with the participants, becoming fluent in each other's histories is the very "bridge-work" (Rowe 2009: 5) needed for acknowledging intersectionality and claiming accountability across lines of power and identity.

Audience members who share personal stories, embody feelings and emotions, and create aesthetic representations within a performance event begin to unseat their privileged position as viewers. In collaborating with youth participants and/or participating in similar activities as them, they move away from their role as merely onlookers. These active frameworks create the conditions necessary for engaging in reflexivity, or a critical examination of "the assumptions underlying our actions, [and] the impact of those actions" (Cunliffe 2004: 407). Reflecting critically on self, others, and society, taking risks, and recognizing relationships between identity and experience can prepare audiences for the work of building alliances with the youth participants. Cultural theorist Homi Bhabha posits that doing this work always invites a negotiation of who we are in relation to others. "[W]hen a new situation, a new alliance formulates itself, it may demand that you should translate your principles, rethink them, extend them" (1990: 216). It is in these moments of relation and negotiation, however small or temporary, that we create the conditions for belonging.

Something is happening here.

Notes

1 While the Tribal Council deliberated, Stephani Etheridge Woodson and I talked with the youth participants about what responsible representation looked like for them, as well as the power inherent in their own stories. As a group, we discussed the potential consequences of sharing the video with a wider audience, changing the video to

address the council's concerns, and keeping their stories the same. In this dialogue, I privileged my ideas of what it meant to be a youth-allied adult, and I didn't fully consider my role as a white-ally to an indigenous community. Moreover, I failed to address with the youth the larger historical, racialized, and systemic oppressions at play in the dialogue and deliberations, as well as the content of their digital stories. Explicitly bringing these contexts into the room for myself and the youth participants is an essential piece of critical pedagogy, as well as building alliances across power lines. It could also be a key framework for responsibly sharing and contextualizing the digital stories with/for public audiences.

2 James Thompson proposes that the face-to-face encounter supports these kinds of affective experiences. "It is in this space that the demand of the face is more likely to be felt. And of course this is the firm ground that on which participatory performance operates" (Thompson 2009: 176).

3 The Performing Justice Project was founded by Megan Alrutz, Kristen Hogan, and Lynn Hoare in 2011. This applied theatre program uses a variety of live and mediated performance tools to explore and enact gender and racial justice with young people. PJP is funded by the Embrey Family Foundation and the Center for Women's and Gender Studies at the University of Texas at Austin.

4 Frameworks based in social media and technology raise concerns around privilege and access and require careful consideration and adaptation based on availability of and access to technology, as well as prior knowledge and experiences of audiences in the room. These activities, like many of those outlined in this book, require adaptation to respond to and include all audience members.

5 In this activity, taking care of your partner means paying attention to physical limitations and restrictions, comfort levels with touch, etc.

6 While I discuss many of these activities as frameworks that I have led, youth often participate in structuring and/or facilitating action frames with the audience. Depending on the time available and the skill set of the youth involved, I work with youth in various ways to determine how the audience could be involved actively in a screening event, as well as what types of activities they would like to engage the audience in. With more experienced participant groups, the youth may fully develop and lead the facilitation of the action frames for an event.

References

Alrutz, M. (2006) "A stream of conscience: Reflecting on ethics and representation in drama with youth," *Teaching Artist Journal*, 4(4): 252–256.

Bhabha, H. (1990) "The third space," in J. Rutherford (ed.), *Identity: Community, culture, and difference*, London: Lawrence & Wishart.

Bharucha, R. (2011) "Problematizing applied theatre: A search for alternative paradigms," in S. Mackey and A. S. Fisher, "Introduction to Rustom Bharucha's keynote lecture: Problematising applied theatre: a search for alternative paradigms," *Research in Drama Education: The Journal of Applied Theatre and Performance*, 16(3): 365–384.

Cunliffe, A. L. (2004) "On becoming a critically reflexive practitioner," *Journal of Management Education*, 28(4): 407–426.

Etherton, M. and Prentki, T. (2006) "Drama for change? Prove it! Impact assessment in applied theatre," *Research in Drama Education: The Journal of Applied Theatre and Performance*, 11(2): 139–155.

Fuchs, T. and De Jaegher, H. (2009) "Enactive intersubjectivity: Participatory sense-making and mutual incorporation," *Phenomenology and the Cognitive Sciences*, 8: 465–486.

Goffman, E. (1974) *Frame analysis: An essay on the organization of experience*, London: Harper and Row.

"Graffiti Alphabet," Drama-based Instruction Network. <http://www.utexas.edu/cofa/dbi/content/graffiti-alphabet> (accessed September 23, 2013).

hooks, b. (1994) *Teaching to transgress: Education as the practice of freedom*, New York: Routledge.

Jackson, A. R. (1997) "Positioning the audience: Inter-active strategies and the aesthetic in educational theatre," *Theatre Research International*, 22(1): 48–60.

Kondo, D. K. (2000) "(Re)visions of race: Contemporary race theory and the cultural politics of racial crossover in documentary theatre," *Theatre Journal*, 52(1): 81–107.

Nicholson, H. (2005) *Applied drama: The gift of theatre*, New York: Palgrave Macmillan.

Norris, M. "About," Race Card Project, online. <theracecardproject.com> (accessed May 28, 2013).

Schechner, R. (2003) "Performers and spectators transported and transformed," in P. Auslander (ed.), *Performance: Critical concepts in literary and cultural studies*, vol. I, London: Routledge.

Taylor, P. (2003) *Applied theatre: Creating transformative encounters in the community*, Portsmouth, NH: Heinemann.

Thompson, J. (2009) *Performance affects: Applied theatre and the end of effect*, Basingstoke, UK: Palgrave Macmillan.

White, G. (2013) *Audience participation in theatre: Aesthetics of the invitation*, New York: Palgrave Macmillan.

Winston, J. and Strand, S. (2013) "Tapestry and the aesthetics of theatre in education as dialogic encounter and civil exchange," *Research in Drama Education: The Journal of Applied Theatre and Performance*, 18(1): 62–78.

Woodson, S. with M. Alrutz, J. Chapman, L. Hager, J. Lazarus, J. Saxton, and M. van de Water (2005) "A matter of ethics: Questions, concerns, and problems in seven voices," *Stage of the Art*, 17(2): 5–10.

5 Performing possibility

"Are you part of a movement?"

At first glance, the gymnasium was unremarkable. It had a high ceiling, concrete floors, gray block walls, and florescent lighting. Every word and movement echoed through the space. The youth participants sat in a semicircle on the floor. My co-facilitators and I vocally performed a few examples of six-word gender stories for the group. Afterwards, I stood in front of the participants, inviting them to think about their own personal stories and experiences related to gender. One of the youths raised her hand. Our eyes met and she started talking: "Can I ask you a question? What are you about anyway? What do you stand for? Are you part of a movement or something?" Her questions hung in the air as twenty-five incarcerated young women, ages 13–18, waited for me to name my politics.

My eyes scanned the gymnasium, looking for an answer, for inspiration, perhaps for permission to speak. Instead, I became hyper aware of how in fact this gymnasium was not like many others: this one had locked doors, guards dressed in military fatigues, and surveillance cameras monitoring and recording the youths' every moment, this moment. *What am I about?* The words repeated in my mind. *Am I part of a movement? How much should I say? How much can I say and still be allowed to do this work here?* My mind was spinning with thoughts of feminist performance pedagogy, anti-racist alliances, and the politics of performance. I wanted to say something about risk and vulnerability, and the challenge of speaking one's truth, particularly in this setting. More specifically, I wanted to dialogue with this group about what it means to be(come) a youth-allied adult and to imagine justice-oriented alliances in this place, this space, and this moment.

In previous chapters in this book, I explore how my approach to digital storytelling as an applied theatre practice with youth presents opportunities for building alliances and enacting justice. I suggest that teaching artists and facilitators (including myself) must imagine new ways of engaging young people and working toward critically engaged practices within and through our creative work. In Chapter 2, I focus on theoretical and practical approaches to building an intentional community of practice and becoming a youth-allied adult when working within a youth-based digital storytelling ensemble. In Chapter 3, I investigate how devising digital stories through social and relational practices can support the building of alliances with and between youth participants themselves. Finally, in Chapter 4, I extend this discussion of alliances by imagining how digital storytelling performances and screenings offer opportunities to engage invited audiences in critical and embodied dialogues with youth performance-makers. Together, these chapters suggest that digital storytelling as an applied theatre practice can work to value the experience and wisdom of young people in several ways. Moreover, they point to how this work can and does create the conditions necessary for becoming an ally and building alliances. However, they also point to some of the complex sets of power relations that exist within applied performance programs with and for youth, and the need for facilitators to address multiple relations and lines of power.

Toward coalitional consciousness

The questions raised in the youth prison remind me that power and politics (including our personal ideologies) are always at play in my (our) work—whether it gets named or not. In this final chapter, I reflect on the notion that building and bridging alliances across these three diverse groups—namely youth, facilitators, and intergenerational audiences—should include the explicit naming of the politics underpinning our pedagogy and practice. Moreover, I suggest that creating and sustaining such alliances requires attention to what Cricket Keating calls "coalitional consciousness-building"[1] or "engendering solidarity across multiple lines of difference" (2005: 86–87).[2] Building coalitional consciousness, then, necessarily includes efforts to pursue and value the tensions and discomfort that often arise from acknowledging power and difference. Inspired by the work of Keating (2005), and other feminist scholars such as Chela Sandoval (2000), Amie Carillo Rowe (2008), and Ann Russo (2013), I imagine how digital storytelling as an applied theatre practice with youth might explicitly take on the practice of coalitional consciousness-building, and thus efforts toward collective accountability to one another.

In her often-cited article "Building Coalitional Consciousness," Keating emphasizes coalitional consciousness "as a set of understandings, motivations, and ways of seeing that can be constructed, formed, and fostered together" (2005: 94). To develop such practices, Keating encourages groups of women, and I suggest groups of youth participants and intentional communities of practice, to engage in the following steps:[3]

> Step One: Locating Experience
>> In a small group that meets regularly, share experiences relating to a chosen theme, paying close attention to the national, racial, class, and other relevant contexts and histories in which the experiences being articulated are being played out.

Step Two: Seeing Resistance to Multiple Oppressions
Examine the experiences with an eye for the multiple relations of
oppression and resistance at play.
Step Three: Coalitional Risk-Taking
Explore the barriers to, and possibilities for, coalitional action with
regards to the experience. What are the power relations among
women themselves [or individuals in the group] that must be challenged in order to build and sustain coalitional action?

(2005: 94)

Speaking to Rowe's (2008) invitation to become fluent in one another's histories, Keating encourages groups to share stories and acknowledge different
experiences. In addition, her article offers reflection questions that can help
youth explore how power functions in and across their experiences, as well as
the threads of oppression and resistance at play across their stories. Keating
titles her final step with the acknowledgement that this methodology requires
risk-taking (2005: 94). Specifically, participants working to build coalitional
consciousness must be willing to look at, name, and disrupt their own relationships to power and privilege. By looking at "differential relations of power
operating in the world as well as the ways that [individuals] are differentially
implicated in any given situation" (Russo 2013: 42), the group is able to explore
collective strategies for resisting various lines of oppression, while attending to
individual contexts. Ultimately, this work focuses attention not only on difference but also on its relational nature and political possibilities.

Politics of performance

In many ways, this deceivingly simple practice of sharing and analyzing
personal stories constitutes a significant political act. As youth participants
begin to recognize personal stories, individual differences, and lived experiences as valuable forms of knowledge, they disrupt traditional social expectations and hierarchical ways of making meaning. After all, political
coalitions are often built on the basis of similarities rather than differences,
and official and valued forms of knowledge tend to be based in science rather
than experience. Simply practicing Keating's methodology often begins to
disrupt the status quo.

In my experience, much of the performance work created with and for youth
does not address identity politics or identity-based differences in a direct or
significant way. Reoccurring and often hidden and systemic efforts to depoliticize our engagements with youth means that many young people, as well as
adults, lack models for attending to power, identity, and difference.[4] Keating's
methodology, and the very naming of coalitional consciousness-building efforts,
encourages more explicit engagements with youth participants about the politics of performance and media, as well as their own storytelling work. Her
theory and practice acknowledge the generative power of personal stories and

experiences. Moreover, they offer pathways to gain perspective and imagine coalitional acts of resistance.

Digital and performance-based practices, such as those outlined throughout this book, offer additional opportunities to explore the relationships between identity, experience, and power. When employed in conjunction with Keating's steps, these aesthetic and embodied tools become explicitly critical frameworks for engaging young people. In turn, these frameworks can help develop youth's (and facilitators') consciousness around power and the production of knowledge in and through our lives.

The promise of possibility

As I conclude this book, I am aware of the many challenges around facilitating digital storytelling as an applied theatre practice with youth. This work raises difficult questions about negotiating individual and systemic oppression in youth's lives, as well as local and global strategies for resistance. I often struggle to address overarching ideals and goals for justice, while simultaneously responding to the local cultures, identities, and contexts of individuals, communities, places, or spaces. I see the need to expand alliances beyond youth's communities of practice and invited audiences, as well as address the risks involved in public, artistic engagements. Often, the very individuals who need to hear youth's stories or whose cooperation is required to enact youth's vision for coalitional action are not in our creative spaces or visiting our screenings and presentations. Moreover, young people are often required to collaborate, work, study, and live within the very systems that perpetuate oppressive norms and identity-based inequities, such as racism and sexism. How, then, can we invite and support young people to challenge these systems, such as schools, while working successfully within them? Inviting or supporting young people to disrupt the status quo comes with risk and consequences that need to be made visible and fully considered by everyone engaged in the practice. As in my digital storytelling work on the Rez, in schools, and at the prison, those risks and consequences are not always visible or clear-cut.

Finally, digital storytelling as an applied theatre practice with youth continues to raise questions about quality, ownership, and access. How might creative practices with young people work to disrupt narrow or hegemonic assumptions and values around quality, ownership, and access? As facilitators work to respect the wisdom and experience of youth, how might we expand measures or notions of what constitutes good or quality art in work with young participants? What new models can we create around authorship and ownership that truly value collaborative endeavors and take into account the intellectual and artistic property generated by young people within participatory performance programs? What efforts can we make to disrupt traditional power dynamics between adult facilitators, youth performance-makers, and invited audiences? Addressing each of these areas, in theory and practice, constitutes a political act—acts that are necessary for changing the ways young people are valued and engaged in society.

The constant work of becoming an ally requires attention to these questions—to the politics of performance, as well as our lived experiences. In digital storytelling work with young people, becoming a youth-ally means building relational practices, including a willingness to see inequities and cultivate an awareness of self and others. Moreover, this work requires critical and embodied performance practices that recognize and value difference—because it is through understanding difference and its relational nature that we (the big we) are able to build stronger models for equity and justice. As part of my own practice of becoming an ally, I want to engage young people in performance practices that matter, in a movement toward possibility.[5] The vision for that promise cannot be mine (ours) alone.

I am in a youth prison. Can I say that I am here to work against identity-based inequities at play in our lives—many of which are alive and well in this system, this place? Can I say that I am trying to build feminist, anti-racist alliances with young people? Can I move past my own fear and discomfort and get these words out of my mouth? I took my eyes off the surveillance cameras and looked back at the young participants sitting on the gymnasium floor. My lips began to move:

> I am interested in making the world different—better—with and for young people … I believe that violence, poverty, and injustice are often perpetuated in response to difference. I believe—I know—that getting to know each other's experiences and investing in each other's differences is one way to start making a world that I want to live in. We can start with knowing and valuing each other's stories. Yeah, I guess I am part of a movement—to use story and performance to create the kind of just world I want to live in. What kind of world do you want to live in?

"What are you about?" … She made me think.

Notes

1 I first encountered the phrase "coalitional consciousness" in Aimee Carrillo Rowe's (2008) book *Power Lines: On the Subject of Feminist Alliances*. Coalitional consciousness has roots in the feminist consciousness-raising movements and has since been theorized by scholars such as Chela Sandoval (2000), Adela C. Licona (2005), and Cricket Keating (2005) among others.

2 Keating (2005) and Sandoval (2000) suggest that coalitional consciousness-building involves intentionally working against simplified celebrations of unity—a critique of early feminist movements—and toward alliances that actively value differences across race, class, sexuality, and other identities.

3 Cricket Keating credits Chandra Talpade Mohanty, Maria Lugones, and Bernice Johnson Reagon with inspiring her methodology. She writes, "The approach itself is based on the radical democratic practice of feminist consciousness-raising, yet

reconfigures the method in several ways in light of critiques by women-of-color feminists" (2005: 87).

4 I argue that efforts to depoliticize work with and for youth can result from adults' discomfort with acknowledging our own power, as well as discussing contested topics such as class, race, sexuality, and ability. Moreover, efforts to remain apolitical might arise from fear of having to make real changes in our own lives to achieve justice and equity.

5 As I do in Chapter 3, here I invoke scholar Della Pollock, who argues, "Performance is a promissory act. Not because it can only promise possible change but because it catches its participants—often by surprise—in a contract with possibility: with imagining what might be, could be, should be" (2005: 2).

References

Giroux, H. (1992) *Border crossings: Cultural workers and politics of education*, New York: Routledge.

Hesford, W. S. (2009) *Identities: Autobiographies and the politics of pedagogy*, Minneapolis: University of Minnesota Press.

Keating, C. (2005) "Building coalitional consciousness," *NWSA Journal*, 17(2): 86–103.

Licona, A. C. (2005) "(B)orderlands' rhetorics and representations: The transformative potential of feminist third-space scholarship and zines," *NWSA Journal*, 17(2): 104–129.

Pollock, D. (ed.) (2005) *Remembering: Oral history performance*, New York: Palgrave Macmillan.

Russo, A. (2013) "Between speech and silence: Reflections on accountability," in S. Malhotra and A. C. Rowe (eds.), *Silence, feminism, power: Reflections at the edges of sound*, Basingstoke, UK: Palgrave Macmillan, 34–49.

Sandoval, C. (2000) *Methodology of the oppressed: Theory out of bounds*, Minneapolis, MN: University of Minnesota Press.

Appendix A
Online resources categorized by topic

Audio tools

Audacity. Online. Available HTTP: http://audacity. sourceforge.net/ (accessed July 15, 2013)

> Audacity is free downloadable software for recording voice-overs. In addition to recording voice-overs, users may edit tracks and layer in music or sound effects.

American Music Company, Inc. Online. Available HTTP: http://american musicco.com/register/ (accessed July 12, 2013)

> On American Music Company, Inc., users can search thousands of copyrighted songs by description or genre, and save potential songs in a project folder before downloading. This site requires membership.

Freeplay Music. Online. Available HTTP: http://www. freeplaymusic.com (accessed July 12, 2013)

> Freeplay Music offers a large searchable database of copyright-free music, and does not require membership to download files.

Sound Jay. Online. Available HTTP: http://www.sound-jay.com (accessed July 12, 2013)

> Sound Jay offers a searchable database of copyright-free soundbites, including some music as well as commonly sought-after animal noises, human noises, and so forth.

Vocaroo. Online. Available HTTP: http://www.vocaroo.
com (accessed July 12, 2013)

> Vocaroo is a free and easy-to-use online tool to record
> student voice-overs. While it does not contain tools to edit
> or add music to voice-overs, it can be used for the initial
> voice recordings, and can be emailed or downloaded.

Classroom management tips

Banaszewski, T. (2002) *Digital Storytelling Finds Its Place in
the Classroom*, MultiMedia & Internet @ Schools. Online.
Available HTTP: http://www.infotoday.com/MMSchools/
jan02/banaszewski.htm (accessed July 12, 2013)

> Banaszewski writes from an educator's perspective,
> offering advice for classroom management techniques
> while recording voice-overs and using iMovie. This
> article is supplemental food for thought for someone
> who already has knowledge of facilitating digital
> storytelling in the classroom.

De Craene, M. (2006) *Digital Storytelling: A Practical
Classroom Management Strategy*, the Educational Technology: ICT in Education. Online. Available HTTP:
http://terry-freedman.org.uk/artman/publish/printer_804.php
(accessed July 12, 2013)

> As an educator, De Craene offers practical tips for
> delegating tasks and keeping students on progress when
> creating small group digital stories with large classes.
> This article is appropriate for an educator who already
> understands the digital storytelling process and needs
> ideas for classroom management.

Collections and samples of digital stories

Center for Digital Storytelling. *StoryCenter YouTube
Channel*. Online. Available HTTP: http://www.youtube.
com/user/CenterOfTheStory (accessed July 14, 2013)

The Center for Digital Storytelling provides examples of work created by workshop participants on this YouTube channel. Many of the works are not created by youths, yet they offer insight into how varied the content and purpose of digital storytelling can be, approaching topics such as war refugees, human rights, race, and bullying.

Creative Narrations. *Digital Story Collection.* Online. Available HTTP: http://www.creativenarrations.net/stories (accessed July 15, 2013)

Creative Narrations works with educational institutions and non-profit organizations to create digital stories to tell personal narrations and build community. Its gallery of digital stories features work by both youth and adults, including works by youth about issues such as domestic violence and community change.

CreativeWorks. Online. Available HTTP: http://www.creativeworksstudio.org (accessed July 12, 2013)

CreativeWorks, located in Kansas City, offers applied theatre programming to marginalized teenagers; the organization's website includes examples of digital stories created by youth with an emphasis on social change and the integration of both photography and video.

Digital Storytelling in the Scott County Schools. (2010) Online. Available HTTP: http://www.dtc.scott.k12.ky.us/technology/digitalstorytelling/ds.html (accessed July 12, 2013)

This site offers examples of digital stories created by K-12 students in Scott County, Kentucky over an eight-year period. The stories address topics such as family, life lessons, and culture.

LaGuardia Community College. *Digital Storytelling: Sample Projects.* Online. Available HTTP: http://www.laguardia.edu/dstory/stories.htm (accessed July 15, 2013)

> LaGuardia Community College's Digital Storytelling course is developed to help English-language-learning adult students build their communicative skills. Its website features student videos exploring immigration and personal stories.

Llano Grande Center. *Digital Storytelling School Kit: Now Showing.* Online. Available HTTP: http://captura.llano-grande.org/showing.html (accessed July 14, 2013)

> The Llano Grande Center provides multiple examples of digital stories developed by individuals and small groups, ranging from middle school students to adults. The topics include family histories, personal stories, and school and community issues.

Porter, B. *The Art of Telling Digital Stories.* Digitales. Online. Available HTTP: http://digitales.us (accessed July 12, 2013)

> Digitales provides resources on creating and evaluating digital stories, and offers a myriad of youth-created examples of digital stories to foster social change, confidence, and identity. The site offers fresh ideas for digital storytelling projects, such as pieces where the writer imagines how he or she will be successful in the future and writes from that perspective.

Silence Speaks. (2010) *Case Studies.* Online. Available HTTP: http://www.silencespeaks.org/case-studies/50.html (accessed July 15, 2013)

> Silence Speaks works internationally with survivors of violence and abuse, war, or displacement. The survivors write and create digital stories about their lives, with examples of works told in languages other than English and works that incorporate illustrations, as well as photographs and videos.

Stories for Change. Online. Available HTTP: http://www.storiesforchange.net (accessed July 15, 2013)

> Stories for Change is a site where digital storytellers can publish their stories, providing a wide variety of digital stories published by all ages and about a variety of community and social concerns. The website serves as both a great database to search digital stories, and a valuable resource for publishing and sharing work.

Streetside Stories. *Student Stories*. Online. Available HTTP: http://www.streetside.org/stories/index.htm (accessed July 15, 2013)

> Streetside Stories works in schools in the San Francisco and East Bay area, focusing on underserved schools, to provide students with digital storytelling experiences to promote literacy and the arts, and build community. Its site offers a sampling of work developed by K–12 students.

Wales Art. (2013) *Your Video*, BBC. Online. Available HTTP: http://www.bbc.co.uk/wales/arts/yourvideo (accessed July 15, 2013)

> Wales Art began the "Your Video" initiative to collect digital stories made by individuals of all ages (both with or without workshop training) to reflect the diversity and capture the personal stories of Welsh individuals. Videos include transcripts of the stories and interviews with the storytellers, making this source a valuable tool during the script-writing and storyboarding process.

Comprehensive resources

Center for Digital Storytelling. Online. Available HTTP: http://www.storycenter.org (accessed July 11, 2013)

The Center for Digital Storytelling (CDS) offers expert resources on digital storytelling. Their website includes information and publications on the steps and philosophy behind the CDS digital storytelling process, as well as details on international digital storytelling projects, events, and professional development opportunities for educators and the general public. The site also offers links to many digital stories on topics from healthcare to family.

Levine, A. (2010) *50+ Web 2.0 Ways to Tell a Story*. Online. Available HTTP: http://50ways.wikispaces.com (accessed July 11, 2013)

Levine offers a large database of storytelling prompts and exercises, sources for copyright-free visual and audio media, and online tools to compile and edit digital stories. This site is valuable for individuals wishing to gain a broad understanding of digital storytelling, as well as those looking for specifics to aid in the process.

Llano Grande Center. *Digital Storytelling Toolkit*. Online. Available HTTP: http://captura.llanogrande.org/index.html (accessed July 14, 2013)

The Llano Grande Center defines the multiple roles and tasks required to complete a digital story and provides multiple examples. This site is a handy resource for those facilitating digital stories with youth, as it includes sample parental consent forms, and other such legal considerations.

University of Houston Education. (2013) *Educational Uses of Digital Storytelling*. Online. Available HTTP: http://digitalstorytelling.coe.uh.edu/index.cfm   (accessed July 15, 2013)

The University of Houston Education Department's comprehensive website provides educators with an overview of digital storytelling; tips for successful writing, planning, and creating of digital stories; sample lesson plans and rubrics; and examples of student work. The site also provides a detailed list of software for both Mac and PC computers, including an explanation of the purpose and value of each software program.

Copyright and ethics

Center for Digital Storytelling. *Core Principles for Ethical Practice in Digital Storytelling*, Online. Available HTTP: http://www.storycenter.org/ethical-practice (accessed July 13, 2013)

The Center for Digital Storytelling offers compelling points to consider regarding protecting the storyteller in the process of creating a digital story, from considering the storyteller's emotional well-being to giving them control over how their story develops, how and if their identity is used, and how and if their story gets shared.

Creative Commons License Explained. Online. Available HTTP: http://www.youtube.com/watch?v=4ZvJGV6YF6Y (accessed July 13, 2013)

This video explains how Creative Commons licenses allow artists to use one another's work, and the limitations that may exist depending on the agreement, such as whether or not users can modify the work, or use it commercially. This video is written at a level appropriate for middle and high school students.

Faden, E. *A Fair(y) Use Tale*. Online. Available HTTP: http://www.youtube.com/watch?v=CJn_jC4FNDo (accessed July 13, 2013)

Faden explains fair-use copyright law (that is, where small excerpts of copyrighted material may be used for education purposes, parody, and other uses). The video playfully incorporates Disney clips, and the information is presented at a level appropriate for middle and high school students.

Rosenzweig, R. *Digital Storytelling: Navigating Copyright Issues*, Center for History and New Media. Online. Available HTTP: https://sites.google.com/site/chnmdigital-storytellingaha2012/navigating-copyright-issues (accessed July 13, 2013)

> Rosenzweig offers educators and digital story creators a clear explanation of copyright infringement, Creative Commons, and fair use as they apply to educators and the classroom.

Curriculum

Alrutz, M. (2011) *Digital Storytelling, Learning through Arts and Technology: An Online Professional Development Program for Teachers*, Florida Alliance for Arts Education. Online. Available HTTP: http://www.faae.org/learning-through-arts-and-technology-digital-storytelling#ab (accessed August 15, 2011)

> Alrutz provides educators with a basic introduction to digital storytelling, including vocabulary, sample lesson plans and practices, suggested supplies, and additional resources.

Creative Narrations. *Digital Storytelling Train the Trainer Institute: Instructor's Guide*. Online. Available HTTP: http://www.mappingvoices.org/sites/default/files/pages/MOVEInstructors_GuideSm.pdf (accessed July 24, 2013)

Creative Narrations outlines a curriculum for a three-day intensive workshop in digital storytelling, which can be modified to fit the traditional school-day schedule. The curriculum includes activities, worksheets, and tips.

Microsoft in Education. *Digital Storytelling in the Classroom*, Online. Available HTTP: http://www. microsoft.com/education/ww/teachers/guides/Pages/Digital-storytelling.aspx (accessed July 24, 2013)

Microsoft in Education provides an editable rubric to evaluate a finalized digital story, as well as a self-reflection tool for students to evaluate their final product and overall process.

Ohler, Jason. (2013) *Resources: Handouts, Presentations, How-tos*. Online. Available HTTP: http://www.jasonohler.com/resources/handouts.cfm#storytelling (accessed July 24, 2013)

Ohler provides handouts and PowerPoint presentations on storyboarding, developing stories, and assessing stories. His documents also include a section titled "Assessing Technological Impact" to encourage users to evaluate the purpose and power of technology.

Public Broadcasting Service. *Place-Based Digital Storytelling Modules*, Online. Available HTTP: http://www. pbs.org/nationalparks/for-educators/digital-storytelling (accessed July 24, 2013)

PBS offers unique digital storytelling curriculum using Google Earth to create digital stories about locations, inspired by Ken Burns's film *The National Parks*. Three modules are provided to accommodate different levels of experience, technology capabilities, and time constraints.

Trowbridge, T. *Multimedia Storytelling (Language Arts, Art, Film)*, Public Broadcasting Service. Online. Available HTTP: http://www.pbs.org/americanfamily/teacher3.html (accessed July 12, 2013)

> Trowbridge offers ideas on getting started with a digital storytelling unit through this broad curriculum, which includes skills developed and considerations for what types of technology to use, and alternatives to technology if it is not available in the classroom.

Digital editing tools

Bosch, K. *et al*. *Digital Storytelling with the iPad*. Online. Available HTTP: https://sites.google.com/site/digitalstorytellingwiththeipad/home (accessed July 11, 2013)

> Bosch and a team of educators created this easy-to-follow website to make digital storytelling more accessible to all users. Applicable to iPad users, this website compares apps that enable digital storytelling.

Instructional Technology Services. *Guidelines for Shooting Effective Video*, Online. Available HTTP: http://its.ksbe.edu/dst/projects/GuidelinesforShootingVideo.htm (accessed July 14, 2013)

> The *Guidelines for Shooting Effective Video* Power-Point provides quick and accessible tips to improve camera-work, suitable for use in instruction with middle and high school students.

PrimaryAccess, Center for Technology and Teacher Education, Curry School of Education at the University of Virginia. Online. Available HTTP: http://www.primary-access.org/ (accessed July 12, 2013)

> PrimaryAccess is an effective and free online tool, offering students the ability to plan for, script, storyboard, and create a digital story all on one website. The website includes searchable photographs of historical events and figures.

Digital storytelling sharing tools

Creative Narrations. (2009) *Promoting Your Stories*. Online. Available HTTP: http://www.creativenarrations.net/sites/default/files/creative_narrations_promoting_stories2.pdf (accessed July 15, 2013)

> Creative Narrations outlines tips for sharing digital stories, encouraging digital storytellers to see the potential for their work to impact a community and create change. This handout includes a brainstorm for planning a screening of stories, as well as documenting the success of screenings.

Intersect. Online. Available HTTP: https://intersect.com (accessed July 24, 2013)

> Intersect is an online database of photos, videos, and stories, that enables users to search for posts by location and by keywords.

Mapping Desire. Online. Available HTTP: http://www.utexas.edu/cofa/mappingdesire (accessed July 24, 2011)

> Mapping Desire provides an example of how Google Maps can be used to house and share a variety of audio stories created by multiple users.

Roadside Theater. *Story Banking Tutorial*. Online. Available HTTP: http://roadside.org/asset/story-banking-tutorial?unit=256 (accessed July 24, 2013)

> Roadside Theater created a video tutorial on how to create and manage a story bank, which is an online or offline resource created by a group or individual to store stories with a related theme to share with the community.

Digital storytelling steps

Lambert, J. (2010) "Seven Steps of Digital Storytelling: Core Methodology of the Center for Digital Storytelling," Prezi. Online. Available HTTP: http://prezi.com/j0ag7l5pr0yl/seven-steps-of-digital-storytelling (accessed July 13, 2013)

> In this great resource for beginners, Lambert introduces the seven steps of digital storytelling as defined by the CDS in this visual presentation, which includes video components of digital stories created by workshop participants at the center.

Photography tools

bigfoto. Online. Available HTTP: http://www.bigfoto.com (accessed July 12, 2013)

> At bigfoto, users can search and download high-quality Creative Commons photographs to incorporate in their digital stories.

Flickr. Online. Available HTTP: http://www.flickr.com (accessed July 12, 2013)

> While the Flickr database includes many photographs not available for public use, an advanced search reveals many photographs labeled for Creative Commons usage.

Getty Museum Education Staff. *Lesson Plans*, The Getty. Online. Available HTTP: http://www.getty.edu/education/for_teachers/curricula/esl2/esl2_lesson_plan_index.html (accessed July 24, 2013)

> The Getty visual arts curriculum includes two lessons in photography using professional photographs. Suitable for middle and high school students, the lessons include extension activities to incorporate hands-on learning.

GIMP. Online. Available HTTP: http://www.gimp.org/ (accessed July 15, 2013)

> GIMP is a powerful and free photo-editing software available to download online. While GIMP can be a difficult tool to learn, it provides high-quality photo editing similar to costly alternative software.

Rowse, D. *13 Lessons to Teach Your Child about Digital Photography*. Online. Available HTTP: http://digital-photography-school.com/13-lessons-to-teach-your-child-about-digital-photography (accessed July 24, 2013)

> Rowse provides thirteen concise and easy-to-grasp tips to improve photography, with example photographs and additional material for each tip.

Recommended equipment

Alrutz, M. (2011) *Digital Storytelling, Learning through Arts and Technology: An Online Professional Development Program for Teachers*, Florida Alliance for Arts Education. Online. Available HTTP: http://www.faae.org/learning-through-arts-and-technology-digital-storytelling#ab (accessed August 15, 2011)

> Alrutz provides educators with an introduction to digital storytelling, associated vocabulary, sample lesson plans, suggested supplies, and additional resources.

Llano Grande Center. *Digital Storytelling Toolkit: Setting Up a Technology Infrastructure*. Online. Available HTTP: http://captura.llanogrande.org/appendix2.html (accessed July 14, 2013)

> The Llano Grande Center provides a detailed explanation of what equipment is required to begin digital storytelling, suitable for the user getting started with digital storytelling.

Ohler, J. (2013) *Storytelling and New Media Narrative: Technology, Techniques, Resources*. Online. Available HTTP: http://www.jasonohler.com/storytelling/storytech. cfm (accessed July 14, 2013)

> Ohler speaks to both the necessity of technology and the practicality of using what is easily available, making this guide to equipment helpful for a user with a limited budget.

Storyboarding tools

Digital Storytelling in the Classroom, Microsoft in Education. Online. Available HTTP: http://www.microsoft. com/education/ww/teachers/guides/Pages/Digital-storytelling. aspx (accessed July 24, 2013)

> Microsoft in Education provides downloadable storyboarding templates, as well as detailed steps in how to create a student-friendly storyboard in Microsoft Word.

Ohler, J. *Digital Storytelling Storyboard Templates*. Online. Available HTTP: http://www.jasonohler.com/pdfs/storyboard_template.pdf (accessed July 14, 2013)

> Ohler's storyboarding template is modified to suit the needs of a digital storytelling project, and includes clear and easy-to-follow instructions for use.

PrimaryAccess, Center for Technology and Teacher Education, Curry School of Education at the University of Virginia. Online. Available HTTP: http://www.primary-access.org (accessed July 12, 2013)

> PrimaryAccess is an effective and free online tool, offering students the ability to plan for, script, storyboard, and create a digital story all on one website. The website includes searchable photographs of historical events and figures.

Sheppard, J. (2009) *Josh Sheppard*. Online. Available HTTP: http://www.thestoryboardartist.com/Site/Home.html (accessed July 14, 2013)

> Sheppard, a professional storyboard artist, shares images of the storyboard work he has done for television and film. This easy-to-navigate resource will help digital storytellers see how to articulate visual components of a story during the planning process.

University of Houston Education. (2013) *Digital Storytelling: How to Create Storyboards*. Online. Available HTTP: http://digitalstorytelling.coe.uh.edu/page.cfm?id=23&cid=23&sublinkid=37 (accessed July 14, 2013)

> The University of Houston Education Department defines the purpose of storyboarding in a concise and easy-to-understand article, which includes multiple downloadable storyboarding templates and links for additional resources.

Theatre and community-building activities

Farmer, D. (2010) *Drama Resource*. Online. Available HTTP: http://dramaresource.com (accessed July 12, 2013)

> Farmer provides theatre educators with games to develop theatre skills and build community for all ages, grouped according to skills developed.

Improv Encyclopedia. Online. Available HTTP: http://improvencyclopedia.org (accessed July 14, 2013)

> The Improv Encyclopedia provides easy-to-follow instructions to over 500 games, many of which are not just limited to training in improvisation. Games are organized into categories, with categories such as Icebreakers and Warm-ups that will aid in developing theatre skills and building community.

MacDonald, S. and Rachel, D. *Augusto Boal's Forum Theatre for Teachers (Notes from a Workshop at Athens Conference 2000)*. Online. Available HTTP: http://organizingforpower.files.wordpress.com/2009/03/games-theater-of-oppressed.pdf (accessed July 24, 2013)

> MacDonald and Rachel detail the notes from a workshop with Augusto Boal, founder of Theatre of the Oppressed. The notes include several of Boal's games for building community and trust.

Sotto, T. *Five Easy Drama Games for the Early Elementary Classroom*, Kennedy Center ArtsEdge. Online. Available HTTP: http://artsedge.kennedy-center.org/educators/how-to/tipsheets/five-easy-drama-games.aspx (accessed July 14, 2013)

> Sotto details five games that can be used with early elementary students, providing explanations of the theatre skills addressed, including memorization, projection, movement, and character choices.

Spolin, V. (1986) *Theater Games for the Classroom: A Teacher's Handbook*, Northwestern University Press. Preview online. Available HTTP: http://books.google.com/books/about/Theater_games_for_the_classroom.html?id=_Cp-xvnCEgIC (accessed July 24, 2013)

> Spolin's landmark book of theatre and community-building games can be explored online and then purchased for future use. Suitable games for all age groups are categorized by type, and include instructional strategies and sample teacher dialogue.

Theatre Games, TheatreTeachers.com. Online. Available HTTP: http://www.theatreteachers.com/theatre-games (accessed July 14, 2013)

> TheatreTeachers.com offers a database of theatre games, categorized by age, group size, or content.

Wiener, D. (2013) *Improv Games: Story-Making, Constructing Alternative Realities, Part 2 of 3*, Rehearsals for Growth. Online. Available HTTP: http://www.rehearsalsforgrowth.com/improv6.html (accessed July 24, 2013)

> Wiener details improv exercises that focus specifically on developing storytelling skills, while still working on ensemble-building and other theatre basic skills.

Writing and story-generating tools

Creative Narrations. (2009) *Story Triggers*. Online. Available HTTP: http://www.creativenarrations.net/sites/default/files/creative_narrations_story_triggers2.pdf (accessed July 15, 2013)

> In this handout, Creative Narrations's simple list of story prompts are broad enough to generate diverse responses from users, while specific enough to help get to the heart of a story.

Iredell-Statesville Schools. *Personal Narrative Prompts*. Online. Available HTTP: http://www.iss.k12.nc.us/curriculum/sallred/pnprompts.htm (accessed July 24, 2013)

> Iredell-Statesville Schools provide a list of meaningful writing prompts to help students develop personal narratives that will lend themselves to impactful digital stories.

Roadside Theater. *Story Circles*. Online. Available HTTP: http://roadside.org/samples/story-circles (accessed July 24, 2013)

> Roadside Theater uses story circles to create an intimate and safe space where participants can share personal narratives. The site includes guidelines to facilitating an effective story circle.

Storybird. Online. Available HTTP: http://www.story-bird.com (accessed July 24, 2013)

> Storybird combines visual arts and technology to help students create illustrated stories and poems, useful for prompting creative writing and as an introduction to the storyboarding process. The site also provides ways to share and offer peer feedback on stories.

University of Houston Education. *How to Write a Script*. Online. Available HTTP: http://digitalstorytelling.coe.uh.edu/page.cfm?id=23 (accessed July 24, 2013)

> The University of Houston Education Department offers examples of writing prompts, tips for peer feedback, and explanations of story structure and story mapping, as well as additional resources to aid in the story-writing process.

Appendix B
Select glossary of terms

Assets

The digital items collected or created for a digital story, including the voice-over, digital photographs, video clips, music, and sound recordings.

Devising

The process of remembering, creating, performing, and/or documenting a story or performance.

Digital story

A two– to three–minute personal story, or "movie," that includes a narrated voice-over and photographs or video, as well as music or sound.

Editing

The process of digitally arranging, altering, or combining assets to create a digital story.

Final cut of digital story

The final cut of a digital story includes all of the participant's desired assets: digital images or video, music, voice-over, etc., and refers to a complete and fully edited digital story.

Moments of knowing

Times within the collaborative, aesthetic process where a common understanding develops among participants, or new ideas come to light for the group within the creative process.

Moving image

A digitally recorded video, animation, or other digital documentation that includes changing elements.

Narrative

The words of, or script for, a digital story voice-over.

Performing

To use one's body, face, and/or voice to deliver a story, line of dialogue, gesture, or meaning. In digital storytelling, we often use the word "perform" to refer to the delivery of a narrative or voice-over, i.e. to perform one's voice-over.

Pitch

A formal presentation of stories, images, ideas, or a storyboard for a group with the expectation of feedback.

Shooting

Filming or digitally capturing photos and/or video.

Soundtrack

The music or sound effects that underscore a digital story.

Still image

A digitally recorded photograph, drawing, collage, etc. that does not include video, animation, or other moving elements.

Storyboard

A visual representation, outline, or map of a digital story. The storyboard usually includes different tracks that represent how various pieces of the digital story will line up and progress throughout the story: the visual elements, the words of the voice-over, the music, and sound effects.

Tableau

A frozen image or picture, created with the body or a group of bodies.

Transition

A visual process for moving from one digital image or video sequence to the next.

Voice-over

The recording of a storyteller's voice narrating a story.

Appendix C
Select theatre, media, and storytelling activities

These activities have been adapted from a variety of print and online sources, as well as learned in multiple training and production settings over the course of many years in the field. I've made efforts to cite my sources where possible and apologize in advance if the source was unknown.

Branches of Significance

This activity offers a starting point for remembering life-changing events and visually brainstorming ideas for a digital story. Invite participants to draw or map out a timeline of their life by drawing a tree with a tall trunk. Encourage participants to mark significant moments in their lives with branches that split off from the main tree trunk. Ask participants to indicate at least three to five of the most significant crossroads, or moments of decision in their lives, by drawing branches to the right and left of the main tree trunk and labeling them with a word or phrase that represents their significant moment. (For example: "Parents Divorced" or "Won Soccer Match" or "Became a Big Sister.") The lowest branches indicate significant moments from the participant's youngest years and the top branches represent more recent moments.

Check-ins

This ritual offers an opportunity for participants and facilitators to gather in the playing space and quickly establish how people are doing. Invite participants to stand or sit in a circle and share a word or phrase indicating how they are feeling and/or what emotional or physical state they carried into the space. As an alternative, invite participants to indicate how they are feeling by demonstrating a thumbs up, thumbs sideways, or thumbs down. Participants can always choose to pass if they are not comfortable sharing.

Circle Center

This ritual offers a way to begin and end a session as a group. I use the term "circle center" to invite a group to come together and stand or sit in a circle. The spatial arrangement helps ensure that everyone can be seen and heard.

Cover the Space

Invite participants to move around the room silently, trying to cover or walk over every inch of the playing space. As the participants move through the space, covering the entirety of the room, invite the group to pay attention to their breathing and their pace. After a few minutes, add a second and simultaneous challenge for the participants to evenly spread themselves out in the room. The group continues to walk and move through space while attempting to fulfill these two objectives related to covering the space. (Adapted from Boal 1992; Rohd 1998; Spolin 1986.)

Cover-the-Space Challenges

Once participants have explored moving their bodies through space, "Cover the Space" introduces certain commands or challenges as the participants move around. For example, invite the group to "Stop" (which means to freeze), "Go" (which means to move again), "Hands" (which means to raise both hands in the air and then bring them down), "Knees" (which means to tap their knees), "Jump" (which means to briefly jump in place), and "Name" (which means to say your name out loud). Once the commands have been shared and mastered by the group, invite further focus from participants by mixing up the commands. For example, if the facilitator says "Stop" they actually mean "Go." If the facilitator says "Hands," they actually mean "Knees." This activity helps build ensemble, listening skills, and cooperation among participants. (Adapted from Boal 1992; Rohd 1998; Spolin 1986.)

Creative Digital Self-Portraits

In this digital media activity, participants capture digital self-portraits or photographs of themselves that do not include the face and at the same time communicate something important about themselves. An example might be a photograph of an open hand holding a key or a full-length mirror reflecting an open window. Digital self-portraits encourage participants to think creatively about visual composition and what visual images might communicate their core values, personal characteristics, or skills. This activity works well in pairs and small groups.

Cross the Line if ...

For this activity, participants stand in a line facing the facilitator. The facilitator reads out statements, such as "Cross the line if you are an only child." Anyone for whom the statement applies leaves the line and steps forward. After each round, the initial line is re-established and everyone stands together again, and the facilitator reads a new statement such as "Cross the line if you think voting matters." This activity offers a way for participants to get to know each other and can prompt youth to consider their own lives in context with others. (I learned this activity from Amanda Hashagen during our Inside OUT program.)

Gesture of Sharing

Through a facilitated moment of exchange, participants share something about themselves, often by sharing pieces of their creative work—even if that work is still in process—with other individuals in a group. The simple exchange of ideas, stories, images, or objects, coupled with group reflection and feedback, fosters a sense of reciprocity and relational practices between participants.

Graffiti Alphabet

On a large sheet of paper or a series of small sheets of paper, participants use markers to reflect and brainstorm on a topic, reading, image, or story. Once the theme is established, the participants draw and write words, phrases, and images related to the main topic that start with each letter of the alphabet ("Graffiti Alphabet"). Encourage participants to visually represent their point of view through their drawings, font choice, line weight, etc.

Heads Up, Heads Down

Participants stand in a circle. When the facilitator says "Heads down," everyone looks at the floor. When the facilitator says "Heads up," participants look up, directly at another participant's face. If two people happen to be looking at each other at the same time, one of the following can occur:

(1) The two participants run to the center of the circle and high-five or greet each other.

(2) The two participants step back and are eliminated from the round. The final participant(s) left in the circle is the winner(s).

This activity can break the ice with a new group or offer a fun warm-up for a community of practice. (I learned this version of the activity from Michael Rohd.)

Hot Seating

In this activity, a participant sits in a chair in front of the audience. The audience is invited to interview or directly question the individual. The participant usually responds to the questions in character or as the storyteller, and occasionally chooses to simply consider and reflect on questions without responding to them in the moment. This technique is used to prompt the individual or the audience to explore a person's background, history, reasoning, or beliefs, as well as to help flesh out details or contexts of their personal story.

I Am Poem [template]

This poetry structure invites writers to fill in a template, sharing personal characters about themselves. I Am Poems might lead to embodied frozen images or digital images that represent how individuals think, feel, and look. Prompts like "I am _____" invite participants to explore a variety of personal assets and to end up with a poetic piece of reflective writing. Many templates exist online for engaging people in creating an "I Am Poem," and young people often enjoy the fast and poetic results from filling out an "I Am Poem" template about their own lives.

I Come from a Place [prompt]

This prompt can be explored both literally and figuratively, as well as in writing or out loud. Invite participants to respond in writing to the prompt "I come from a place ..." as many times as they can in five minutes. Exploring concrete answers to this prompt might lead to answers, such as "I come from Orlando, FL," or "I come from my house." Abstract answers might include "I come from a place where no one carried cell phones," or "I come from a place with the smell of citrus and orange blossoms." (I learned this prompt from storyteller Jon Spelman.)

Improvised Story Circles

Improvised Story Circles can help build storytelling skills. A variety of activities fall into the category of story circles. For example, in one word storytelling, participants sit in a circle and tell a story as a group. One at a time, each person in the circle contributes one word, building on the previous words and the story at hand. This activity can also be done by inviting each person to add simple phrases or sentences to collectively build a longer improvised story. This activity can invite reflection around story structure and collaboration as well. For a more structured framework, invite participants to begin a story circle with one of the following phrases:

a. Once upon a time …

b. Every day …

c. But then one day …

d. And because of that …

e. And because of that …

f. And because of that …

g. Until finally …

h. And ever since then …

"It Made Me Think" [prompt]

Use this prompt to invite participants to reflect on a digital storytelling session, a moment, or a larger experience by completing the phrase "… It made me think." Invite participants to communicate an idea, with one word or phrase, that will stay with them after the session has ended. For example, after a session on digital editing, someone might reflect: "Digital assets, it made me think." Or after a session someone might recall someone's story that addressed the complexity of citizenship and say, "Living the 'American dream,' it made me think." Participants' distilled reflections are shared out loud, but are not explained. (I learned this prompt in a workshop with Michael Rohd.)

People to People

Invite participants to stand back to back with a partner. As the facilitator calls out two body parts, such as "hand and elbow," participants turn toward their partner and silently touch their hands to their partner's elbow. As the game progresses, introduce combinations that require greater risk or intimacy, such as "hand to smaller back," "toes to toes," "pointer finger to nose," or "forehead to forehead." As participants become more comfortable with the game, they often lose their inhibitions and become more willing to take creative risks. When the facilitator calls "people to people," participants quickly find a new partner, and the activity continues with a new set of body parts.

Photo on the Wall

Hang a variety of photos on a wall. Invite participants to move through the room, browsing the photos before they choose one image that resonates with them. Once participants choose a photo, ask questions to prompt reflection, such as "What is going on in this image?" "What might you have in common with the person in your photo?" "Where do you think the person in the image lives and why?" The content of the photo can become a springboard for reflecting on identity and social location, and eventually for devising a story, scene, or monologue.

Spectrum of Difference

This activity invites participants to think critically about their point of view. As various statements are read out loud, participants respond to the statements by placing their bodies on an imaginary line, or spectrum, in the room. They move to one end of the line to signify their agreement or an affirmative response to the statement read, or to the other end of the line to signify disagreement or a negative response. The participants embody their individual responses to the statements and collectively demonstrate a spectrum of responses among the members of the group.

Storyboarding

A storyboard is a linear, visual map of a digital story and can be completed at various stages in a project, including early on as a tool for brainstorming visual assets, in the middle of the process as a tool for organizing and assessing assets, or near the end of the project as a map for editing final assets together. Participants create storyboards to demonstrate how they will combine a story narrative with visual images, transitions, sound, or music to create a digital story. Participants often use PowerPoint, index cards, or pre-made templates for storyboarding (see resources in Appendix A for links to worksheets and storyboarding templates).

Story Circle Pitches

Once participants decide on the story they want to develop, a story circle can help them pitch their idea to a small group or the entire class. Ask the group to sit in a circle and allow each participant 2–3 minutes to share the main ideas, dramatic question, and possible structure of their story. Allow another 2–3 minutes for the listeners to ask questions and/or offer feedback about what stands out for them from the story. I love to close by inviting people in the circle to share images that each story evoked for them.

Think, Pair, Share

Offer participants a topic or question to consider. Give them 20–30 seconds to think about it on their own. Next, invite them to find a partner or a small group and to share their ideas with each other. Finally, invite each pair or small group to share out one big idea from their discussion to the larger group.

Timed Storytelling Activities

Timed storytelling activities require participants to choose the first idea that pops into their head. This helps participants turn off their inner critique and follow their instincts. Invite participants to work in pairs to tell a story in 3 minutes, then 2 minutes, then 1 minute, then 30 seconds, then 10 seconds, and finally 2 seconds. This exercise in repetition and concision helps participants determine what is most important in their story, as well to recall new and specific details with each retelling.

The Truth about Me [prompt]

This theatre activity can also be used as a writing prompt. Invite participants to stand or sit in a circle with one participant in the center. The person in the center completes the phrase "The truth about me is ..." with a true statement about themselves. They might share a truth about a food they like, something they are wearing, or a personal characteristic. For example, "The truth about me is that I like the color blue." When the statement is made out loud, all of the participants in the circle who agree with the statement cross the circle and move to a new spot. At the same time, the person in the middle tries to get out of the middle by obtaining a spot in the circle. Whoever does not gain a spot in the circle goes to the center and the game begins again. Facilitators might encourage people to share truths that are not outwardly visible as a way to deepen the experience. Depending on the group, facilitators may need to mark "spots" around the circle with chairs or tape on the floor.

Vote from Your Seat

Read a statement or a question to the group and invite participants to vote, or demonstrate their response, with their bodies. In this activity, participants express their opinion or point of view by standing up to express agreement, sitting down to express disagreement, and standing with a knee on a chair for an in-between response. If time permits, invite a few participants to explain their vote or point of view to the group.

References and resources

Boal, A. (1992) *Games for actors and non-actors*, New York: Routledge.

"Graffiti Alphabet." *Drama-based instruction network.* <http://www.utexas.edu/cofa/dbi/content/graffiti-alphabet> (accessed September 23, 2013)

Neelands, J. and Goode, T. (2000) *Structuring drama work: A handbook of available forms in theatre and drama*, 2nd edn., Cambridge: Cambridge University Press.

Rohd, M. (1998) *Theatre for community, conflict, and dialogue*, Portsmouth, NH: Heinemann.

Spolin, V. (1986) *Theatre games for the classroom: A teacher's handbook*, Evanston, IL: Northwestern University Press.

Index